Dedicated to all the teachers who
educated, motivated and helped shape
me into the person I am today.

-A.N.

Hidden throughout this book are 5 hidden boogers.
See if you can "pick them out" while you read!

MiLo Ink Books
www.miloinkbooks.com

The Girl Who Lost Her Voice / by Adam T. Newman; illustrations by Susan G. Young
Text copyright ©2016 by MiLo INK Books / Adam T. Newman
Illustrations copyright ©2016 by Susan G. Young
All rights reserved.

ISBN-13: 978-0-9910909-4-5
ISBN-10: 0-9910909-4-2

Printed in China by Gold Printing Group
First edition

VERMONT DOLLARS, VERMONT SENSE

A Handbook for Investors, Businesses, Finance Professionals, and Everybody Else

BY MICHAEL H. SHUMAN
& GWENDOLYN HALLSMITH

Foreword by STUART COMSTOCK-GAY

A PROJECT OF POST CARBON INSTITUTE,
VERMONTERS FOR A NEW ECONOMY, GLOBAL COMMUNITY INITIATIVES,
THE PUBLIC BANKING INSTITUTE, AND THE FRESH SOUND FOUNDATION

Interior design: Girl Friday Productions
Development and partnerships: Ken White
Editing and production: Daniel Lerch

ISBN-13: 978-0-9895995-3-5
ISBN-10: 0989599531

Post Carbon Institute
613 Fourth St., Suite 208
Santa Rosa, California 95404
(707) 823-8700

www.postcarbon.org
www.resilience.org

Image credits: cover, upper left image © Erika Mitchell (via Shutterstock), other images as noted below; page 19, courtesy of City Market; page 23, courtesy of SunCommon; page 33, courtesy of Vermont Creamery; page 37, courtesy of Gwendolyn Hallsmith; page 50, courtesy of Real Pickles; page 53, courtesy of Opportunities Credit Union; page 71, courtesy of UVM Special Collections.

Special thanks to John Burt and the Fresh Sound Foundation for providing the funding for this handbook. Additional research and writing assistance was provided by Matt Napoli, now a graduate of St. Michael's College.

Post Carbon Institute's mission is to lead the transition to a more resilient, equitable, and sustainable world by providing individuals and communities with the resources needed to understand and respond to the interrelated economic, energy, and ecological crises of the 21st century.

ABOUT THIS HANDBOOK

This is the first in what we hope will be a series of state-specific handbooks to spur local investment across the United States. Each handbook will be filled with local examples and information, modeled on this first edition focused on local investing in Vermont.

Vermont is an appropriate place to start this series. Vermonters have long been mindful about preserving their small communities, and protecting and strengthening the local businesses that give their communities such unique character. One of the ways they have done this is by voting with their wallets. Data from the U.S. Department of Agriculture show that Vermonters purchase the most local food per capita in the country. Vermont's chapter of Businesses for Social Responsibility has the most members of any state—not just per capita, but in total. Small, local businesses are still the rule in Vermont, rather than the exception. Travel down just about any Main Street in the state and instead of a long line of predictable, anywhere-ville national chains, you'll find door after door of proud local stores.

Vermont also enjoys a rich assortment of financial innovations, which are presented in the case studies that follow. Its historic culture of frugality, self-reliance, and creativity led entrepreneurs like Ben Cohen and Jerry Greenfield to finance their new ice cream business with a 1970s equivalent of crowd-sourced financing: Vermont everyday investors were given the opportunity to buy local stock in the company. This same trend continues today: the state's new crop of cyber-geeks is designing crowdfunding platforms; the state's largest city, Burlington, is using its bonding authority to make sure affordable housing is available for its residents; and the state is leveraging its own bank deposits to make it possible for businesses to invest in renewable energy.

If you are interested in sponsoring a handbook like this for your own state, please contact Ken White at Post Carbon Institute, ken@postcarbon.org.

PARTNERS

Post Carbon Institute
http://www.postcarbon.org

Vermonters for a New Economy
http://www.facebook.com/
VermontCoalitionForANewEconomy

Global Community Initiatives
http://www.facebook.com/GlobalCommunityInitiatives

The Public Banking Institute
http://www.publicbankinginstitute.org/

The Fresh Sound Foundation
http://freshsoundfoundation.org/

ABOUT THE AUTHORS

Michael Shuman

Michael Shuman is an economist, attorney, author, and entrepreneur. He's also an adjunct instructor at Simon Fraser University in Vancouver, a Fellow at Cutting Edge Capital and Post Carbon Institute, and a founding board member of the Business Alliance for Local Living Economies (BALLE). He has authored, coauthored, or edited nine books, most recently *The Local Economy Solution: How Innovative, Self-Financing Pollinator Enterprises Can Grow Jobs and Prosperity* (Chelsea Green, 2015). One of his previous books, *The Small Mart Revolution: How Local Businesses Are Beating the Global Competition* (Berrett-Koehler, 2006), received a bronze prize from the Independent Publishers Association for best business book of 2006. Over the past 30 years, Shuman has lectured in 47 U.S. states and eight countries, giving an average of more than one invited talk per week. He blogs regularly at michaelhshuman.com.

Gwendolyn Hallsmith

Gwendolyn Hallsmith, is the founder and Executive Director of Global Community Initiatives and one of the founders of Vermonters for a New Economy, both non-profit organizations based in Vermont. She is the author of *The Key to Sustainable Cities: Meeting Human Needs, Transforming Community Systems* (New Society, 2003);

a workbook with World Resources Institute and Earth Charter USA called *Taking Action for Sustainability: the EarthCAT Guide to Community Development*; a workbook with Hunter Lovins and Natural Capitalism called *LASER: Local Action for Sustainable Economic Renewal*, and *Creating Wealth: Growing Local Economies with Local Currencies* and *Community Currency*, both with Bernard Lietaer.

Gwendolyn has over 25 years of experience working with municipal, regional, and state government in the United States and internationally. She has served as the Planning and Community Development Director for the City of Montpelier, the Town Manager of Randolph, Vermont, the Regional Planning Director in Franklin County, MA, a Senior Planner for the Massachusetts Executive Office of Energy Resources, and the Deputy Secretary of the Vermont Agency of Natural Resources. Her international experience has included work with the United Nations Environment Program, the United Nations Development Program, the Institute for Sustainable Communities, the International City/County Management Association, and Earth Charter International.

FOREWORD

By Stuart Comstock-Gay

Reading this book, I am reminded of the power of community.

One of the great challenges of life in the 21st century is capturing that sense of community. We live in a world that is simultaneously larger and smaller. It's larger in that we have opportunities to experience so much more than ever before. We can travel, move, see and experience things that would have been unimaginable to our ancestors. Our vistas of the world are bigger. But it's also a smaller world because while we can see so much more, it often seems that our ability to control our lives—our sphere of influence—is ever reduced. It's that latter point that troubles me. We all need to have hope that what we do matters.

We all need a sense of community. And we all need to believe that we have agency—a sense that we can make choices that will affect our lives.

This book captures an entire set of efforts that seek to restore our sense of agency and hope and community. By using our financial resources to invest in our neighbors and their works—whether in small businesses or to support housing projects, or so many other things—we can begin to recapture our communities, and our sense of community.

The reality of the modern world is that activities in China and Turkey and Somalia matter for us in very real ways. And part of our attention will necessarily be on the broader world. But we must also find ways to re-invest in, and commit to, our local communities. "There's no place like home," said Dorothy. "So why not invest in it?" says this book.

Stuart Comstock-Gay is President and CEO of the Vermont Community Foundation.

CONTENTS

INTRODUCTION 1

THE CASE FOR INVESTING LOCALLY 3
   1. Why should we care about local business? 3
   2. Are local businesses competitive and profitable? 5
   3. Why are Americans underinvesting in local business? 7
   4. What are the contours of the emerging local investment revolution? 9
   5. What are the risks and returns of investing locally? 10

A QUICK PRIMER ON LOCAL INVESTMENT 13

TOOLS FOR GRASSROOTS INVESTORS 15
   1. Personal Finances 16
   2. Cooperatives 18
   3. Local Bank or Credit Union 20
   4. Self-Directed IRA 22
   5. Pension Fund 24
   6. Local Investment Club 26

TOOLS FOR LOCAL BUSINESSES 29
   1. Conventional Sources 30
   2. Accredited Investors 32
   3. Program Related Investments 34
   4. Cooperative Options 36
   5. Pre-Selling 38
   6. Sponsorship Websites 40
   7. P2P Lending Sites 42

8. Employee Stock Ownership Plans 44
9. Private Offering 46
10. Direct Public Offering 49

TOOLS FOR FINANCE PROFESSIONALS. 51
1. Credit Union 52
2. Targeted CDs. 54
3. Federal Programs 56
4. Local Investment Fund 58
5. Local Stock Market 60
6. Local Mutual Fund 62

MULTI-CONSTITUENT TOOLS 65
1. Investor Networks 66
2. Community Lists 68
3. Slow Munis 70

LEGAL AND REGULATORY ACTION 73
1. The JOBS Act and State Securities Reforms 74
2. State Funds 76
3. Public Banking 78

RESOURCE LIST 80

ENDNOTES 81

INTRODUCTION

A powerful "local economy movement" is now sweeping across the United States and around the world. More than a thousand American cities and towns have local business networks or related projects led by such groups as the American Independent Business Alliance (AMIBA), the Business Alliance for Local Living Economies (BALLE), and the Main Street Program of the National Trust for Historic Preservation. Organizations like Transition Network and Slow Food are engaging tens of thousands of other communities worldwide. In all of these places people are attempting to strengthen local businesses, promote "buy local" campaigns, and end subsidies and other unfair advantages given to nonlocal businesses.

One motivation spurring this movement is concern about climate change. Businesses, institutions, and individuals are divesting from fossil fuels and looking for genuine alternatives to the carbon-intensive companies that dominate the global marketplace. They are not satisfied with taking investment away from Exxon Mobil and simply moving it to global firms that depend on fossil fuels to support globe-spanning manufacturing and distribution networks.

Another motivation is fear of financial loss. During the financial crisis of 2008 and the years that followed, stock markets, home values, and job opportunities all plummeted. Growing public distrust of Wall Street launched movements like Occupy Wall Street and Move Your Money, the latter of which organized more than a million Americans to switch from megabanks like Bank of America to local banks and credit unions. Over the same period a grassroots group promoting investment in local food businesses, Slow Money, developed chapters in twenty cities, and has moved $38 million into more than 350 small farms and local food businesses.

That said, local investment is still in its infancy. It can and should be significantly larger than it is today. That's why we have prepared this handbook. We want to show as many people as possible—starting in the United States, state by state, and then perhaps even outside the United States— how they can invest locally. The amount of money at stake for local economies is staggering: if everyday Americans took advantage of the opportunities now available for local investing, at least $15 trillion of capital currently invested on Wall Street could be moved to Main Street.

First, we review the arguments for investing locally— which are made at length in books like *Locavesting* and *Local Dollars, Local Sense*.[1] Specifically, we answer the following questions:

- Why should we care about local businesses?
- Are local businesses competitive and profitable?
- Why are Americans underinvesting in local business?
- What are the contours of the emerging local investment revolution?
- What are the risks and returns of investing locally?

Then in the remainder of the handbook we present tools for local investment, organized into five areas:

1. Tools for grassroots investors looking for local business opportunities.
2. Tools for businesses looking for local investors.
3. Tools for finance entrepreneurs looking to start local investment institutions.
4. Multi-constituency tools which could be used by anyone, including grassroots activists.
5. Legal and regulatory reforms that states can undertake to support all the above tools.

THE CASE FOR INVESTING LOCALLY

1. Why should we care about local business?

Most of us know—or think we know—what the word "local" means. But since there's no precise definition of the word in our language or our law, it's helpful to point out that "local" contains two different concepts: ownership and proximity.

Locally owned businesses are those in which the majority of owners live in the same geographic area where the business is based. Local ownership can come in many forms, including local corporations, nonprofits, employee ownership, and co-ops. Regional chains can be local, but national chains cannot. Franchises that allow the owner/operator a lot of latitude over an outlet's design and supplies could be considered local, but those with encyclopedic top-down requirements (such as McDonald's) would not. Whatever the uncertainty that remains in this definition, one distinction is absolutely clear: *Public companies traded on the New York Stock Exchange or the NASDAQ cannot be considered local.*

Local investing also implies proximate investing—that is, the investors in a business live close to the business they are investing in, usually in the same neighborhood, city, state or region. Proximity confers many benefits on an investor-business relationship, but let's just mention one immediately. While it's impossible for you to meet with the CEO of Walmart, you certainly can meet with the CEO of a local business. You can chat with the staff about the company. You can test out the product or experience the service. By "ground-truthing" the company before you part with your money, your chance of being taken in by a huge, Enron-like swindle is much lower.

Perhaps the single most compelling reason for growing public support of local business is their positive impact on jobs. A terrific website called YourEconomy.org presents one of the richest and most nuanced sources of data on the relative impact of locally owned versus nonlocal businesses.[2] If you look up job growth in the United States between 2008 and 2013, you will find that all jobs in the country grew at a paltry rate of 0.8 percent. Locally owned businesses increased jobs during this period by 1.2 percent. Nonlocal businesses actually *reduced* their jobs by 4.3 percent.

Several recent studies confirm the job impacts of local business:

- A 2010 study appeared in the *Harvard Business Review* under the headline "More Small Firms Means More Jobs."[3] According to the authors, the study shows that "regional economic growth is highly correlated with the presence of many small, entrepreneurial employers—not a few big ones."
- A more recent study just published in the *Economic Development Quarterly*, a journal long supportive

of giving "incentives" to nonlocal business, had a similar finding: "Economic growth models that control for other relevant factors reveal a positive relationship between density of locally owned firms and per capita income growth, but only for small (10-99 employees) firms, whereas the density of large (more than 500 workers) firms not owned locally has a negative effect."[4]

• Still another paper, recently published by the Federal Reserve in Atlanta, looked at counties across the United States and found statistically significant "evidence that local entrepreneurship matters for local economic performance... [T]he percent of employment provided by resident, or locally owned, business establishments has a significant positive effect on county income and employment growth and a significant and negative effect on poverty...."[5]

Local businesses deliver many other benefits to communities besides jobs:

• *Prosperity*—Because local businesses spend more of their money locally, they generate a stronger "economic multiplier effect." Studies show that every dollar a consumer spends at a local business tends to generate two to four times the income, taxes, and charitable contributions as a dollar spent at a comparable nonlocal business.[6]

• *Social Mobility*—Local businesses expand opportunities for entrepreneurship, which then provide market-based ladders for the disadvantaged to move out of poverty.

• *Tourism*—One-of-a-kind stores, restaurants, and shops give a community character and often attract nonlocal customers.

• *Smart Growth*—The smaller size of local businesses can facilitate mixed-used neighborhoods and walkable communities.

• *Social Responsibility*—The presence of local owners also means they are more susceptible to pressure by other stakeholders—consumers, investors, workers, suppliers—for responsible corporate behavior. A recent study sponsored by the U.S. Environmental Protection Agency, for example, found that when you compare two smokestack factories, an absentee-owned factory emits fifteen times the pollution of a locally owned one.[7]

• *Civil Society*—Decades of sociological research shows that communities with a density of local businesses have a stronger civil society, and that community members are more involved in politics, volunteership, and citizen-led change.[8]

All these economic and non-economic benefits together can help communities achieve perhaps their most important goal in the 21st century: *community resilience*. With climate change already occurring, the era of cheap fossil fuels ending, and multinational corporations enjoying greater immunity from national (let alone local) regulation, communities face unprecedented environmental, economic, and social challenges for which they are largely

unprepared.[9] Local businesses, and the localized economic systems in which they operate, are essential to help communities inoculate themselves from these crisis through greater self-reliance.

Ultimately, "local" is all about building a community economy made up of humane relationships. As Michelle Long, executive director of BALLE, says, "The point of local is being able to put a human face behind the transaction. Money is nothing but the moving current beneath us, showing what we care for."

2. Are local businesses competitive and profitable?

Broadly speaking, U.S. local businesses have done remarkably well at competing with global corporations, and two basic facts underscore this conclusion:

- First, if local businesses were becoming less competitive, we would have seen jobs shift from the local half of the economy to the nonlocal half over the last few decades of economic globalization. In fact, when the spectacular growth of home-based businesses in the United States is properly accounted for, there has been no such shift whatsoever. Despite receiving little government support, local businesses have steadily maintained their "market share" of employment.
- Second, if local businesses were becoming less competitive, their profit rates would be lower than those of big businesses. Yet the most recent tax

data available from the Internal Revenue Service show that in 2008, sole proprietors (which most small businesses either are or start out as) generated eleven times more net revenue per sales dollar than C-Corporations. In Canada (where the business climate is not wildly dissimilar from that in the United States) businesses with ten to twenty employees are the most profitable, with margins 63 percent higher than big businesses.[10]

These generalizations, of course, mask important exceptions. Some small businesses have had enormous difficulty competing against bigger businesses. For example, the proliferation of shopping malls and chain stores has certainly killed many small retailers over the past few decades. But retail looms especially large in our consumer consciousness, because brick-and-mortar stores are where we purchase most of our daily goods. In fact, retail only accounts for about 7 percent of the economy.

People sometimes assume that small businesses have high failure rates and are therefore poor investments. But they are probably thinking about just a tiny subset of small businesses—namely *startups*. And indeed, according to the Small Business Administration, about half of all business establishments fail within five years of birth and two-thirds fail within ten.[11] But data from the Kauffmann Foundation, the nation's leading philanthropic supporter of entrepreneurship, show that a typical jurisdiction in the U.S. economy generally can be expected to lose 16 percent of its existing jobs in a given year—which means that the other 84% is stable. Moreover, the same jurisdiction can be

expected to gain 18 percent more jobs in a typical year. A risk-averse local investor might focus on those local businesses that have operated profitably and grown steadily for five to ten years.

Local small businesses have remained competitive in an environment where public officials and economic developers have essentially tried to kill them. A survey recently completed of the three largest economic-development programs in 15 states found that 80% were giving most of their money to attract and retain global business; about a third gave well over 90% of their funds.[12] The impact of these subsidies, if not the intent, is to make small business less competitive. And yet the home-grown competitors held their own.

The tilt of public policies against local businesses goes well beyond economic-development subsides. Generations of federal corporate welfare, ranging from tax breaks to outright gifts—and including trillion-dollar military deployments in the Middle East—have made fossil fuels unnaturally cheap. Public infrastructure favoring global trade like highways, airports, and seaports has been generously underwritten by public dollars, while infrastructure supporting local businesses like community parking lots and intra-city transit have been starved. State sales taxes are largely unenforced against internet giants like Amazon. Trade rules ban communities from placing labels on products letting consumers know whether they were made locally. Antitrust laws that once would have forbidden the way that Walmart whipsaws its suppliers have been largely unenforced.

Even if foolish public policies remain in place, deeper trends in the global economy are likely to make local business more competitive in the years ahead. For example, in 1970 services made up 45% of consumer spending. By 2008 they grew to 60%. This trend is mirrored in every industrialized country in the world. As people make more money, they get saturated with "stuff." After you have your second car, your third computer, your fourth television set, it's easier to see the value in spending your next available dollar on more services like education or health care. This trend is great news for localization, because most services are inherently local and depend on face-to-face relationships with people we know and trust.

Meanwhile, local businesses in all industrial sectors are learning how to compete more effectively, and often showing other businesses how they can be profitable and still treat their workers, suppliers, and the environment well. Through community-based networks, local businesses are spreading best practices—in service, in technology, in business design, in marketing, in finance—all of which are improving their competitiveness. These businesses are learning how working together can strengthen their hand against global corporations. For years, True Value Hardware stores, all locally owned, have successfully competed against the giant Home Depot chain through a producer cooperative. Tucson Originals is a group of local food businesses in Arizona that collectively buy foodstuffs, kitchen equipment, and dishes to bring down their costs. There appears to be no economy of scale that local businesses cannot realize with the right type of collaboration.

All of this has occurred in a world where the principal fuel for the global economy has been affordable oil. Cheap, plentiful, concentrated, and easily portable oil has heated our homes and offices, propelled our cars and jetliners,

powered our machinery, and brought the entire world into an industrial age. Periodic shortages, such as during the OPEC embargos of the 1970s, and periodic price spikes, such as during the summer of 2008 when gasoline was topping $5 per gallon in some areas, have reminded us of our dangerous dependence on cheap crude. These events, however, provided just a preview of an era we can barely imagine. With reserves of conventional cheap oil dwindling, we're increasingly meeting global demand with expensive unconventional oil, much of which comes from more technologically challenging resources like "deepwater" oil in the Gulf of Mexico, shale oil from the fracked fields of North Dakota and Texas, or low-quality tar sands in Alberta. This means that oil is almost inevitably going to be more expensive in the coming decades. While renewable energy offers a long-term alternative, we will not be able to decouple the vast infrastructure of the industrial world, especially its transportation systems, from fossil fuels overnight.[13]

The features of this post-petroleum era will almost certainly increase the competitiveness of local business. Rising oil prices will benefit community-based energy service companies, solar-equipment installers, and household geothermal services. As more people balk at skyrocketing costs of commuting to work, they will increasingly turn to home-based businesses. And common practices in today's economy, such as Walmart contracting with manufacturers to produce cheap consumer goods in low-wage places like China and shipping them thousands of miles to stores throughout North America, will no longer be tenable.

About a quarter of the goods that we consume are "durable"; that is, things that last for a few years or (if we're lucky) decades. These cars, appliances, gadgets, computers, toys, housewares—all the stuff that in recent years has been largely manufactured abroad—only constitute about a tenth of our total consumer spending. Most of our expenditures on goods are for "nondurables," things that tend to be used or consumed relatively quickly like food, textiles, clothing, office supplies, and paper products.[14]

The distinction on durability is critical, because imports of nondurable goods are particularly vulnerable to rising oil prices. Compared to, say, durables like microchips, the nondurable goods tend to weigh more and contain less value per pound. As energy prices and shipping costs rise, imports of nondurable goods may be among the first casualties. This means that local production of food and clothing coupled with local distribution, for example, will once again be competitive against Walmart importing goods from China. Rising transportation costs will swamp long-shrinking labor costs. Thus, rising oil prices will usher in a local economy renaissance worldwide. Manufacturing of nondurable goods will make a comeback.

So, to recap: Local businesses have held their own against the global competition over the past generation, despite public policies tilted against them. And a number of trends, like the shift to services and rising oil prices, will boost the competitiveness of local businesses even further.

3. Why are Americans under-investing in local business?

If local businesses are responsible for more than half the U.S. economy (in terms of both jobs and output), and if the

sector is highly competitive and profitable, then it's not a huge leap to infer that a healthy capital marketplace would ensure that roughly half our available investment capital would go into the local half of the economy. In fact, very little does.

For example, local businesses receive far less than half of the lending capital from banks. Even though small and mid-size banks account for about a fifth of all the capital in U.S. banks, they are responsible for more than half of all small-business lending. Bigger banks, which control most short-term capital, prefer lending to bigger businesses. From a bank's perspective, if a big loan takes as much work as a small loan while promising bigger payoffs, why not go big?

This capital market failure is even more profound when it comes to long-term securities like stocks, bonds, mutual funds, pension funds, and insurance funds. The holdings that U.S. households and nonprofits have in these categories amount to about $30 trillion—almost four times the size of their banking deposits. And yet *almost none* of this $30 trillion touches local business. If the U.S. capital markets were functioning efficiently, at least half of this sum, $15 trillion, would move from Wall Street to Main Street.

What stands in the way of this shift are obsolete institutions and laws that make local investment extremely difficult and expensive. Securities laws from the Great Depression effectively enacted a system of investment apartheid, with "accredited investors" being able to invest in any business they wish and unaccredited investors being essentially told to stick with Wall Street. Accredited investors comprise the richest two percent of Americans—those who earn more

than $200,000 (or $300,000 with a spouse) or have more than $1 million in assets, excluding one's primary residence. As long as entrepreneurs honestly present their business plans, governance, and numbers, they can easily approach any accredited investor for an investment. The other 98% of us are "unaccredited" and presumed too gullible to invest in a company without receiving a massive amount of legal paperwork. Before a business can make an investment "offering" to even a single unaccredited investor, it must pay an attorney to produce a private placement memorandum and various regulatory filings and documents that could easily cost $25-$50,000 in legal, accounting, and government fees. If a company wants many unaccredited investors, it must create a public offering that could cost another $50,000 or more, and it must make ongoing, exhaustive filings to the U.S. Securities and Exchange Commission (SEC).

The thick offering documents required by securities laws are of little use to the lay person for whom they were written to protect. They are filled with turgid, legalistic prose that largely exists on lawyers' hard drives for every company that comes to them. Besides ensuring full employment for attorneys, securities law has had one clear achievement: it has managed to keep small investors away from small business. Ninety-eight percent of the American public cannot invest in more than half of the economy.

Stunningly, there are some signs that our capital market failure is getting worse. For example, community banks are decreasing in assets and numbers. Over the last 15 years, the number of small banks has dropped by a third; their assets have dropped by half. As the financial crisis unfolded early in President Obama's first term, the newly elected

Democratic majority on Capitol Hill felt compelled to pass the so-called "Dodd-Frank" reform legislation (named for the cosponsors, Senator Chris Dodd of Connecticut and Representative Barney Frank of Massachusetts). Congress imposed stiff new regulations on all banks, with no awareness that these were irritating but manageable for large banks while being utterly unaffordable for small banks. As a result, a heartbreaking new wave of bank consolidation is under way, which will further reduce the capital available for small business.

But there have been some important countervailing trends. Over the past 50 years, modest pieces of legislation have attempted to increase community reinvestment. The Community Reinvestment Act of 1977 put an affirmative obligation on banks to invest more of their capital locally. The 1980s saw the introduction of Community Development Financial Institutions (CDFIs), a program that rewards financial institutions that help economically marginalized people with grants and other benefits from the federal government. The New Markets Tax Credits (NMTC) program established in 2000 incentivizes accredited investors to place capital into low-income communities for seven years.

Note, however, that none of these programs improved the investment opportunities for the 98% of us who are unaccredited.

That's why recent reforms have been particularly important. The federal JOBS Act (JOBS stands for Jumpstart Our Business Sector) could make it easier and cheaper for local businesses to take money from unaccredited investors. President Obama signed this law in 2012,

and onc[...]
rules by [...]
investmen[...]

Thirte[...]
ing process, [...]
Act making [...]
businesses. A[...]
pending. Man[...] ...ake
it cheaper for a [...] ...accredited investors than the J[...] at least one—Maryland's
exemption allowing local businesses to borrow $100,000
from unaccredited residents, who may write checks up to
$100—requires almost no legal work whatsoever. (We discuss the JOBS Act and other state reforms in the Legal and
Regulatory Action section.)

4. What are the contours of the emerging local investment revolution?

The tools presented in the following pages make clear that local investment is not the uncharted territory that many people think it is. Some of these tools, like municipal bonds and credit unions, have been around for years. Others, like donation-based and interest-free crowdfunding, are new but easy.

But for investment apartheid to end, a new generation of tools, like equity crowdfunding, will be needed. The local investment revolution probably will need to pass through four distinct stages:

We have to make it easier and cheaper for
businesses to issue securities to unaccredited
local investors.

- *Stage II:* We have to make it easier and cheaper for those unaccredited investors to trade their shares on local stock exchanges.
- *Stage III:* We have to make it easier and cheaper for unaccredited investors to invest in local investment funds, where financial specialists can perform the hard work of choosing and trading local securities.
- *Stage IV:* We have to make it easier and cheaper for the fiduciary agents running pensions, trusts, and other funds to place unaccredited clients' money into local investment pools.

These four changes, moreover, must proceed more or less in the order laid out above. That is, few fiduciary agents, like pension fund managers, will begin to invest funds locally when there are few local investment funds with a reasonable track record of profitability. Few such intermediaries will be established until there are local exchanges that allow the fund to buy and sell securities (illiquid securities are potentially worthless[15]). And no local exchanges in a region will be set up until there are enough local securities to trade.

This logical sequencing underscores why it's premature to begin with a Stage IV question like "How can I localize my pension fund?" College organizers are admirably pushing for their trustees to divest from fossil fuel companies responsible for greenhouse-gas emissions and reinvest in community businesses, but unfortunately the infrastructure needed for redirecting those investments barely exists. Although these organizers can readily point to carbon-free investments, few of these will be local—at least for a while. We need to be patient. We are barely at Stage I. That sounds like bad news, but five years ago we were not even at Stage 0.

Stages II, III, and IV will be legally challenging. Federal law is clear that the states have concurrent power to set Stage I rules regarding the intrastate issuance of securities, but is less clear about state power regarding intrastate stock exchanges, investment funds, and pension investments. Michigan, for example, just passed a law mandating creation of a statewide stock exchange for local companies, but probably will have to negotiate with the SEC to gain full legal authority for proceeding. A major battle of federalism looms ahead, one that might bring together Locavores on the left with Tea Partiers on the right (they have already worked together during passage of the JOBS Act).

Even if the SEC tries to slow or squelch reform, one can imagine well-established national financial institutions willing to comport with federal regulations to provide local investment innovations. It's not inconceivable, for example, that NASDAQ might create one or more local stock exchanges to diversify its brand, that major investment funds like Calvert might create local investment portfolios, and certain pension funds like Pax World might facilitate institutional investing in local portfolios.

5. What are the risks and returns of investing locally?

If local businesses are as competitive as publicly traded companies and have equal or better profit rates, then there

is no good reason why the investors in local businesses ultimately should not enjoy equal or better rates of return. The key word, however, is *ultimately*. In the absence of local stock markets, for example, it's harder to buy and sell shares of companies, which imposes greater costs on anyone who wants to invest locally. Over time, as local stock markets provide greater liquidity and local investment funds provide greater diversification, this problem should dissipate.

One reason why many investors are skeptical of local investment is that they assume that leaving their money on Wall Street is paying 8-12% per year. In fact, data available from Yale professor Robert Shiller, who recently won the Nobel Prize in Economics, show that the average annual rate of return of the Standard & Poor's 500 index—when dividends are added but inflation is removed—is about 2.7%.[16] Moreover, we know that most mutual funds underperform market averages, and most hedge funds underperform mutual funds. The challenge of local investments beating a 2.7% return each year is not wildly unrealistic. Many co-ops, for example, currently pay 5-8% per year on funds borrowed from their members.

Finance professionals also instinctively believe that local investing is riskier than conventional investing. And there are three good reasons why this is probably true:

- A company looking exclusively for local investors will find fewer of them and be less likely to obtain full funding.
- Investors looking only at local companies will find fewer worthwhile candidates and thus may be more likely to end up with investments that do not meet all their goals.
- Because local investing can mean putting all of one's investment eggs in a single geographic basket, a portfolio of businesses in the same place is vulnerable to the inevitable ups and downs of the local business cycle, as well as other disruptions, like natural disasters.

It's worth noting, though, that all these risks reflect the immature nature of the local investment field. As more investors try to invest locally, more local companies will seek local capital. And as local-business funds form around the United States, a risk-averse local investor could divide her portfolio among these funds in multiple cities around the country (though for some this might no longer constitute local investing).

But there's another side to the risk question. Consider the ways that investing locally actually can bring down risk and improve returns:

- As noted, local investors may be able to obtain better information about potential investments. This explains why community banks that make lending decisions based on real historical knowledge of the borrower have lower default rates than big banks that rely on computerized credit scores.
- Local investors appreciate that the returns from their investment go not just to their own bottom line but also to their community's, with more employment and prosperity, a stronger tax base, better schools, less crime, and so forth. The social

returns, in other words, wind up benefitting everyone—including the investor.

- Local investors tend to be less passive than other investors. Owners of a co-op grocery store, for example, become its best marketers, volunteers, and event participants—all of which increases the probability of the business succeeding and paying a good rate of return.

- Because local businesses tend to spend more money locally, their multipliers naturally improve the prospects of neighboring businesses. So an investment portfolio of local businesses might enjoy the benefits of a positive feedback loop, with all the businesses in the portfolio supporting each other's success.

- And, of course, by supporting local and regional economies, local investing strengthens community resilience, which in turn supports the long-term viability of businesses and investors alike.

The science of local investing is still young. As we develop tools for creating affordable investment vehicles, for evaluating businesses objectively, for making local securities tradable, and for assembling diversified local portfolios, local investors will more easily be able to identify the opportunities with the greatest return and the lowest risk.

A QUICK PRIMER ON LOCAL INVESTMENT

Local investment means putting your capital into a local business, project, or initiative with an expectation of a positive rate of return. The legal term for most investments is *securities*.

The three most fundamental types of securities are:

- *Debt*, where the lender expects repayment of principal plus interest;
- *Equity*, where the stockholder hopes for appreciation of the investment, plus dividends; and
- *Royalty*, where a participant expects to receive a percentage of a company's revenues or profits.

All securities carry many kinds of conditions—perhaps a certain schedule for a debt repayment, specified voting rights for stock, or a maximum payout for royalty payouts. *Convertible notes* can combine these attributes, allowing, for example, a lender to convert debt to stock. Lenders with a *subordinate position* get repaid after those in a *senior position*. Holders of *common stock* can vote for board members, while *preferred shareholders* do not.

The underlying theory of investment is that an investor receives a greater return for greater risk. Thus, federally insured bank accounts pay lower interest than do so-called "junk bonds." Debts secured by a borrowers' property carry lower rates of return than those that are unsecured. But since no one can perfectly predict the future, investors should not be surprised if "safe" investments go bust. Stock sellers, for example, might hawk "value stocks" (for established companies) or "growth stocks" (for entrepreneurial upstarts) without making clear that any of these investments can be losers.

Investing in any one company is usually riskier than investing in a pool. That's why many investors prefer to put their money into funds, where an experienced manager picks companies (hopefully!) wisely. For this privilege, investors must pay the funds a variety of fees. A growing number of investors, mindful that in any given year the vast majority of fund managers underperform the market, choose to place their investments in *index funds* that mimic the overall structure of the market for very low fees

Investors also care about the ability to sell a security, if for example he or she needs to "cash out." This is the characteristic of *liquidity*. Stock markets and bond markets are places with high liquidity where investors can easily buy and sell securities.

In *socially responsible investing,* investors choose businesses that comport with their ethical standards. An investor concerned about climate change might *divest* from fossil fuel companies or *selectively invest* in renewable energy companies. Some socially responsible investors are willing to accept greater social returns (e.g., lower greenhouse gas emissions) in exchange for lower private returns.

Not every investment is legally considered a security. If you invest in yourself (by buying a house) or in your own business, for example, you're not investing in securities. Many types of pre-selling are not considered securities investments either. These non-securities, as we shall see, nonetheless contain important opportunities for local investment.

TOOLS FOR GRASSROOTS INVESTORS

Looking for ways to support your local economy? There are plenty of simple actions you can take right now. You can reorganize your household finances. Or move your money into a local bank or credit union. Or join a local co-op. Or start an investment club. Plus, you can tap your retirement savings for many of these possibilities through a self-directed individual retirement account (IRA).

1. PERSONAL FINANCES

Description

Local investment does not have to mean investing in another company—it can mean investing in yourself, your kids, or your house. In fact, there are many promising places where you can put your money and get a rate of return that beats Wall Street. Remember that the average Wall Street investor is only getting about 2.7% return per year. Even if you set your goal higher—say, 5% return per year—there are many ways you might achieve this on your own. For example, getting rid of credit card balances effectively will pay you 15-30% per year. As the Sage of Omaha, Warren Buffett, says, "Nobody ever goes broke that doesn't owe money."[17]

Another easy way to beat Wall Street is to become a homeowner. A home purchase really delivers two different kinds of valuable rewards. One is that you've got a place to live. Instead of paying a landlord every month, you effectively become your own landlord. Yes, you have a big debt in the form of a mortgage, but as you pay it down, you grow an asset that ultimately eliminates your rent. That asset is your second reward, which you ultimately can liquidate for your retirement. At some point, if you need the cash, you can sell your home and move into a smaller one. Or you can secure a "reverse mortgage" that pays you an income stream and gradually works you out of ownership.

Among the factors that make homeownership a great investment is you can deduct interest payments on your mortgage from your taxes, and once the mortgage is paid you have a house rent-free (after property taxes). Additionally, when you cash out your house, you can enjoy up to $250,000 in gain tax-free. In contrast, when you cash out a 401(k) pension or a traditional IRA, you're fully taxed.

Home investment confers one more indisputable advantage on a local investor. As the principal custodian of your home and a member of your community, you actually have the ability to increase the chances of your investments succeeding. You can improve your house through repairs, additions, and tender loving care. You can help stabilize or increase home values in your neighborhood by supporting the local economy and participating in local schools and culture. When you place your retirement money on Wall Street, in contrast, you only can watch and pray.

Challenges

Many Americans, after suffering through years of stagnant wages and a terrible financial crisis, do not have enough savings for a down payment on a house. As they accumulate any savings, moreover, they are surrounded by finance "experts" who encourage them to put money into their Wall-Street destined 401(k) or IRA. In fact, the smartest move is to ignore the experts, pay down the credit cards, and amass enough of a down payment to get at least a small home.

An Intergenerational Mortgage

The members of one Vermont family (who, in true New England fashion, wish to remain anonymous) recently discovered that they could divest from Wall Street by lending to one another. The older generation needed a safe investment; the younger generation needed housing. The solution was obvious. All it took was for some family members to think more like bankers.

Rather than having their adult children go to a bank for a mortgage, the parents offered to cash out some of their stocks and give their kids a loan. Even in the real estate bubble period of 2004-2008, they realized that they could receive a better return from private mortgage payments than they likely would from either Wall Street investments or bank deposits. Meanwhile, the kids realized that they would pay less than they would for a bank mortgage. And it was all strictly local, since the parents were Vermonters and were not going to resell their children's mortgage on the secondary market.

The parents reckoned that in a worst-case scenario, if they had a sudden need for money for expenses the children would have enough equity in the home to get a conventional mortgage. So even though real estate does not tend to be very "liquid"—it takes lots of time to sell a house—there are ways that a deal like this can cover the expected cash needs of everyone involved.

Fortunately for the family, the stocks were sold in the spring of 2008, before the crash. The cash was then loaned to the children, using the same documents banks do for a mortgage. A schedule of payments was established, with the same front-loaded interest and slowly increasing principal any amortization table can provide. The timing was fortuitous for the parents too, because they now had a steady income stream from the mortgage at the same time as most of their other investments' returns had declined dramatically (their stock market losses during the period were over 25%).

The same framework, of course, can also apply to other areas where a younger generation needs capital. Student loans, although quite attractive at the outset, now often carry draconian payback terms, and young people cannot get out from under the debt even if they go bankrupt. Providing loans to children and grandchildren for higher education, with repayment terms suited to their needs as they start off in new careers, would generate long-term benefits for everyone and help keep the profits local.

2. COOPERATIVES

Description

Consumer cooperatives offer another readily available local investment opportunity for grassroots investors. When you join a co-op, you put your capital into an enterprise that rewards you with discounts and other benefits. Additionally, the more you use a consumer cooperative, the larger your patronage dividend: your end-of-the-year bonus that's the cooperative equivalent of a profit. Add it all up, and you may well do better than Wall Street.

A group of scholars at the University of Wisconsin recently surveyed the landscape of U.S. cooperatives and counted nearly 30,000 cooperatives operating at 73,000 locations.[18] The vast majority are consumer cooperatives, with 343 million memberships (many people belong to multiple co-ops, hence the number of memberships exceeds the U.S. population). Credit unions, which are essentially banking cooperatives, have 92 million members. Electrical utility co-ops reach 42 million Americans. The cooperative sector owns $3 trillion in assets, generates half a trillion dollars a year in revenue, and pays 856,000 people $25 billion in annual wages. Significantly, almost all cooperatives qualify as locally owned businesses.

As a member of a cooperative, other local investment opportunities might become available to you as well. For example, a number of cooperatives borrow money from their members for capital projects at very attractive interest rates. In New Mexico, the La Montenita Grocery Co-op created a revolving loan fund for supplier farmers and other local food producers, in which members could invest.

Challenges

Your local investment opportunities here, of course, are limited by which co-ops operate in your community. Most people can easily find a local credit union and a grocery co-op, but other kinds of cooperatives may be harder to find.

Opportunities to lend to one's cooperative are fewer still. Because such loans are securities, it takes a fairly sophisticated and well-established co-op to perform the necessary legal work. That said, co-ops embrace a solidarity principle of helping other co-ops, which means that once a co-op in your state does the necessary legal work for a loan, it's willing to share it with other co-ops (which can then, with modest edits, make good use of the documents).

City Market Onion River Cooperative

Vermont has many successful consumer cooperatives (see http://coopvt.wordpress.com/vt-co-op-directory for a complete listing). Consider City Market Onion River Co-op in Burlington. City Market gives its members better access to healthy and environmentally friendly food choices, primarily from local farms. Anyone can join. Basic members pay an annual fee of $15. When this annual contribution reaches

$200, the member then holds a full share of the company and gets the full benefits of membership. Co-op members then earn money back on purchases through the annual patronage refund (the amount varies according to the member's annual purchases and City Market's annual profit). In 2014, patronage checks were issued to over 10,000 members, with an average check of $93. This amounted to over $968,000 being recirculated into the community.

According to Allison Weinhagen, Director of Community Engagement: "We currently have 10,883 members. Since they own equity in the co-op, they are not only members but also owners." The co-op members elect a board of trustees to manage the operations of the City Market.

Anjanette DeCarlo says becoming a member at City Market has been a very smart and safe investment for several reasons. To start, while it costs $200 to become a member at City Market, she receives a dividend of about $150 at the end of the year, which is close to a 100% return on her initial investment in just one year. While City Market does not currently ask their members for loans, she says, "If they were to ask me for one, I would invest because I am investing small amounts already and seeing large returns. In addition, it is low risk and in line with my morals because they are supporting the local community."

Another benefit for members is the confidence they feel in the integrity of their food. Most if not all of the food comes from local farms and businesses—like Lewis Creek Farm, which counts City Market as one of its main customers. Every City Market purchase increases the amount of money invested in local farms and businesses.

Cooperatives also confer on members the power to help run the business, which effectively allows members to help ensure that their local investment in the co-op is profitable. City Market has annual meetings, which members attend to voice their personal opinions about the successes or short comings of the co-op.

For more information

Allison Weinhagen, City Market, (802) 861-9750, http://www.citymarket.coop.

10,399 checks head to the post office on patronage refund day.

3. LOCAL BANK OR CREDIT UNION

Description

During the financial crisis, when several large banks jacked up the fees they were imposing on checking accounts, Arianna Huffington (who publishes the popular online news site *Huffington Post*), financial televangelist Suze Orman, Rob Johnson of the Roosevelt Institute, and author/filmmaker Eugene Jarecki teamed up to encourage Americans to "move their money" out of big banks in the name of community revitalization. Hundreds of thousands of Americans, perhaps even millions, did so. Jarecki even made a short film that used clips from "It's A Wonderful Life" to illustrate the problem (see http://www.youtube.com/watch?v=Icqrx0OimSs).

Credit unions are member-owned financial cooperatives; they are not-for-profit and do not have outside shareholders. Instead, excess profits go back to the member-owners in the form of higher saving rates, lower loan rates, and more affordable services compared to offerings from private banks.

The case for moving your money into a local bank or credit union is powerful. A dollar deposited in a local bank or credit union is about three times more likely to be lent to a local business than a dollar deposited in a big, interstate bank. As Stacy Mitchell at the Institute for Local Self-Reliance argues: "Although small and mid-sized banks ($1 billion or less in assets) control only 22 percent of all bank assets, they account for 54 percent of small business lending. Big banks, meanwhile, allocate relatively few of their resources to small business. The largest 20 banks, which now command 57 percent of all bank assets, devote only 18 percent of their commercial loan portfolios to small business."[19]

Studies from sources as varied as the Federal Reserve and Consumers Union suggest that, compared to big banks, regional-scale and community banks pay more interest on savings account, charge lower fees, have lower administrative overheads, and have lower default rates. Plus, they reward customers with the kind of personal service that has all but disappeared from larger banks.

Challenges

If you have just a savings and checking account, moving your money to a local bank or credit union is relatively easy. Many Americans, however, have a variety of credit cards and loans with their banks, which means that changing banks may take a focused effort over many months or even years. Refinancing a mortgage through another bank, for example, can be quite time-consuming.

A mindful local investor seeking to refinance a mortgage through a local bank or credit union also should make another inquiry: Will the institution resell your mortgage to a larger banking institution or repackage it for the secondary market? If the answer is "yes" then the benefits of local banking will be short-lived, and the 30 years of mortgage

interest you'll be paying will instead go to a nonlocal institution. Fortunately, it's usually possible to find a local institution that doesn't resell its mortgages.

The Vermont State Employees Credit Union

The Vermont State Employees Credit Union (VSECU) is currently the only statewide credit union in Vermont (other credit unions, most of them smaller, can be found here: http://www.vermontcreditunions.com/findaVTcu. htm). Since the Great Recession in 2008, membership at VSECU increased by 33% to nearly 57,000 in 2015. Because VSECU is able to offer better rates and lower fees, member households enjoyed tangible benefits in 2014 compared to national averages:[20]

- $1,065,300 more earned in savings because of VSECU's higher deposit rates.
- $1,136,320 more saved in loan payments because of VSECU's lower loan rates.
- $1,278,360 more saved in fees because of VSECU's lower fees.

VSECU has branches statewide, making it highly accessible to members. It offers almost all of the same services and conveniences as a private bank, including savings, checking, mortgages, auto loans, personal loans, and credit cards. It also offers account access services found at private banks, such as mobile and online banking, as well as financial advice and brokerage services to help members with retirement, investment, and insurance needs. In addition, it offers a "VGreen" program to help members achieve home energy savings through lower rates for renewable and energy efficiency improvements and off-grid home mortgages.

For more information

Yvonne Garland, VP of Business Development, Vermont State Employees Credit Union, (802) 371-5197, http://www.vsecu.com.

4. SELF-DIRECTED IRA

Description

Since virtually no pension funds today offer meaningful options for investing in local business, one alternative worth considering is to create your own self-directed IRA. Under existing tax law, you can hire an IRS-licensed custodian who must follow and implement all your investment decisions—including, if you want, local investments. All investors, whether or not they are accredited, can take advantage of this.

Any investments you are permitted to make as an individual are possible with your tax-deferred IRA dollars, with two exceptions: You cannot invest in your own business or your kids' business; and, you cannot invest in your own house or your kids' house. (However, you could invest in your neighbor's house, and your neighbor could invest in yours, as long as it wasn't a *quid pro quo* transaction.)

If you shop around, you should be able to find a licensed custodian who will charge you as little as $200 per year. A list of some licensed custodians can be found here: http://selfdirectedira.nuwireinvestor.com/list-of-self-directed-ira-custodians.

You also might convince your local bank or credit union to provide a self-directed IRA as a service for their customers generally. (General requirements for a financial institution to set up a self-directed IRA can be found with the Internal Revenue Service.)

Challenges

The custodian you hire, by law, cannot provide you with any investment advice (except to let you know if you're violating any of specific rules noted above). That means that you have to do much of the work of finding, vetting, and choosing investments yourself. A self-directed IRA requires a serious time commitment to create your own portfolio.

Also keep in mind that even a $200 annual fee can be a significant drain on your bottom line unless you have a relatively large portfolio. For example, if you have an IRA with $20,000, a $200 fee reduces your annual rate of return by 1%. Some providers charge significantly more—$500-$1,000 per year—and add charges for more exotic transactions such as investing in real estate. Of course, keep in mind that many mutual funds you have now may be charging you fees like these that you're not even aware of!

Investing in the Sun

Portions of this story were provided by the Vermont Community Loan Fund and SunCommon; used with permission.

While it's easy to open an IRA at any bank or credit union in Vermont, making that account "self-directed" requires some additional work. But for SunCommon co-founder and co-president Duane Peterson, the work was worth it.

Duane first arrived in Vermont via Los Angeles in 1996 at the behest of the famous Ben and Jerry, who recruited him to take on the role of their "Chief of Stuff," the company's internal agent for social change. When the company was sold in 2000, Duane was working with the Vermont Public Interest Research Group (VPIRG), the state's largest consumer and environmental advocacy organization.

As Board President at VPIRG, Duane immersed himself in research and advocacy around clean energy. Together with VPIRG staffer James Moore, he "imagined a market solution to climate change." They launched SunCommon to make solar energy more affordable through group net metering, whereby a community of homes can draw their electricity from a group-owned solar array. When SunCommon needed financing for their first solar array project in early 2014, the Vermont Community Loan Fund (VCLF) stepped in to offer local financing.

That's what convinced Duane to figure out a way to redirect his IRA into the VCLF. It was a challenge for Duane to convince the custodian for his IRA, Schwab, to vet the loan fund so that he could self-direct it there, but he persevered and succeeded. He needed to fill out forms to prove to the custodian that the VCLF was a legitimate investment and affirm that Duane was willing to take risk outside the SEC-regulated world. All this work required him to pay extra fees (which is why, historically, self-directed IRAs have only been used by wealthy individuals).

"VCLF is now in my safe investment pool," Duane says. "They have a great track record of supporting what I want to support, while also being successful and paying the money back. But I also want to invest in ways that reflect my values. I'll get some return on investment while promoting values-led endeavors."

For more information

Jake Ide, Vermont Community Loan Fund, (802) 223-4423, http://www.investinvermont.org.

Duane Peterson and the staff of SunCommon

5. PENSION FUND

Description

Very few pension funds currently offer local investment options, but as local investment opportunities spread in the larger economy—and especially as local investment funds get established—this will change. For now, the best you can do is apply pressure. You can write letters to the fund managers or to the top brass insisting that they create a local option, or better still, organize your colleagues to carry out a letter-writing campaign. This is how, over the past 25 years, proponents of "screened" or "impact" investing convinced many pension funds to divest from companies that were conducting business in apartheid South African or manufacturing nuclear weapons.

You might point out that your request is not unprecedented. A few large state employee pension funds have made experimental investments in what they call in-state businesses. Since 1999, the New York State Common Retirement Fund has targeted more than $800 million into in-state investments, including $271 million in 107 companies based in New York.[21] In 2008 the Michigan Retirement System committed $300 million to Invest Michigan!, which contains two funds that support promising companies based in the state. Similar investments have been made by public employee pension funds in Ohio, Indiana, North Carolina, and New Jersey. These "economically targeted investments" have been criticized for their relatively poor performance, but the blame hardly belongs to the "local" character of the investments.[22] Almost all of them went into global companies with few ties to the state save perhaps a headquarters. Pension fund investment in truly locally owned businesses, as defined here, has yet to be tried.

Challenges

Under a federal law called the Employee Retirement Investment Security Act (ERISA), pension fund managers have to fulfill a number of fiduciary duties. Some are straightforward: no stealing, no self-dealing, and report your every investment action often and honestly. More formidable is the duty to exercise a standard of care, skill, prudence, and diligence. Not a few fiduciaries have taken the position that this standard demands that they give their pensioners the options of stocks or bonds—period. Choose between Tweedledum and Tweedledee.

For now, the absence of actual local mutual funds makes arguing about the contours of your representative's fiduciary duties rather abstract and premature. Once more local investment funds are around, employees can begin demanding that their fiduciaries include them on their 401(k) menus. The essential argument is simple: How can you possibly claim to be my fiduciary if you insist on investing my money, against my wishes, in destructive global businesses rather than in the local businesses I care about? You are *my* fiduciary, not Wall Street's.

Burlington's Pension Money Provides Affordable Housing

The Champlain Housing Trust in Burlington provides permanent affordable housing to residents by controlling the land the house occupies and splitting equity ownership to control for speculative market appreciation. It has developed over 600 units of permanently affordable housing since its inception in 1984, when Burlington's Community and Economic Development Office provided a start-up grant of $200,000 to launch the Burlington Community Land Trust (which has since been expanded and renamed the Champlain Housing Trust). The city also supported the trust with funds from its Community Development Block Grant (CDBG) and loans from the municipal employee pension fund.

The pension funds were provided to the trust as loan capital to acquire more property. The trust drew on the funds loan by loan, deal by deal. To keep the funds safe, fund managers lowered the risk by applying fairly conservative loan terms: loan-to-value ratios that mirrored traditional bank mortgages. The pension fund made a seven-year loan repayable with one large "balloon" payment at the end.

Using this model, the city was able to provide the trust a much better interest rate than what other financial institutions were offering (interest rates were very high in the 1980s). The Burlington Savings Bank matched the loan with a new seven-year balloon loan to pay off the pension fund. For this particular project, involving buying up properties as neighborhoods were rapidly gentrifying, the land trust also used CDBG funds obtainable through federal grants.

Municipalities are notoriously risk averse, and even in Burlington there is a lot less activism around pension fund investments and municipal indebtedness than there used to be. For now, the city is no longer making loans through its pension fund. Vermonters might press their pension funds, both public and private, to do more local investments like Burlington did.

For more information

Champlain Housing Trust, (802) 862-6244, http://www.getahome.org.

Grand opening of Champlain Housing Trust's Avenue Apartments project.

6. LOCAL INVESTMENT CLUB

Description

Many of the investment options mentioned above, like a self-directed IRA, require considerable work on your own and require you to assume considerable risk yourself. If you want to share some of the work and the risk, you might consider forming an investment club with an express mission of investing locally.

The SEC exempts investment clubs from formal approval, on one big condition: *Every single member must be actively involved in every single investment decision.* Consensus is not required, just open decision-making. If that criterion is met, a club can pool money from its members, invest in local securities, make profits, and provide its members with a nice check at the end of each year. But as soon as even a single member becomes passive and starts relying on the investment advice of others in the club, legal alarms get tripped.

Clubs must have fewer than 100 members; practically speaking, they probably should have fewer than 30. If you're going to put together an investment club, you want to have a good, working relationship with other members. And you want to have a good time when you meet! If you have too many members, with the requirement that everyone debate every decision, the club could become a bureaucratic nightmare.

One of the first local investment clubs was No Small Potatoes in Maine, launched by the local chapter of Slow Money. It involves about two dozen members, including some unaccredited investors, each of whom has contributed between $5,000 and $10,000 into a limited liability corporation. As a group, they then interview farmers and local food producers who wish to obtain small loans. Slow Money currently has thirteen chapters nationwide that have created investment clubs.

Challenges

Note that unaccredited investors cannot pool their money in an investment club to be treated as a single accredited investor. In fact, if a club has a single unaccredited investor, then it can only invest in businesses that legally can accept money from unaccredited investors. In the case of No Small Potatoes, the club got special permission from the Maine Department of Securities for unaccredited investors to make small loans to struggling farmers and food entrepreneurs.

The White River Investment Club

The White River Investment Club is now being formed by Steve Aldrich as an initiative of an organization called Building A Local Economy (BALE). He wants to start the club with 12-24 investors and a minimum of $50,000 in capital. "We felt like $50,000 was the minimum amount of capital we needed in order to make an actual difference in

local businesses," he says. The club plans to form an LLC and issue 100 shares in late 2015. It will require a minimum investment of $1,000 per share and allow each participant to purchase up to 10 shares for a total of $10,000.

Thus far, Aldrich has faced two challenges. One has been recruiting members. "Finding those committed members is hard," he says, "because in rural Vermont not a whole lot of people are in a financial position to invest."

The other challenge has been preparing the Operating Agreement, which lays out the mission, the types of investments the club will pursue, and the rules for decision-making. Aldrich drafted the document based on one put together by the popular Sprout Lenders club in Boston (http://www.sproutlenders.com). Members of the White River Investment Club have one vote per share when making investment decisions (again, with a maximum of ten shares per member).

One interesting conversation within the emerging group concerns how much risk they are willing to take collectively. Aldrich has found that if the problem is framed simply as risk versus reward, the group is surprisingly willing to expose their principal to risk. The potential of an investment serving the community's well-being increases the risk tolerance even more.

Ultimately, members will be encouraged to create offshoot investment clubs in other Vermont communities so that they do not need to travel great distances.

For more information

Steve Aldrich, White River Investment Club, (802) 234-5140.

TOOLS FOR LOCAL BUSINESSES

Interested in securing local investors for your business? Even if you just look at the usual options—accredited investors, angel funds, venture capitalists—a growing number of investors are interested in local business. So are many community foundations and cooperatives. Plus, there are expanding options for obtaining capital from preselling, donation crowdfunding, and peer-lending sites. And changing laws are making it easier for you to raise capital from unaccredited investors through private offerings, direct public offerings, and equity crowdfunding.

1. CONVENTIONAL SOURCES

Description

If you are like many entrepreneurs seeking capital for your business, you will naturally turn first to yourself. You might choose to not take a salary or to retain company earnings for reinvestment. You might take out a second mortgage on your home or take a cash advance on a personal credit card—in which case you should certainly prioritize doing these things with your local bank or credit union (as discussed earlier). Other sources of local capital that might be available include microenterprise funds, economic development funds, community development financial institutions, community development corporations, or state-specific funds (like the Flex Capital Fund of the Vermont Sustainable Jobs Fund, described on page 76). The U.S. Small Business Administration (SBA) has programs that help shore up loans from nervous banks, though they too require that you put your house on the line.

If you've exhausted these resources, remember that you might approach local friends and family—and if that's not enough, you can always search more widely.

Challenges

The most common sources of capital for early-stage entrepreneurs—second mortgages, credit cards, SBA programs—are all about debt. If you (like many entrepreneurs who barely survived the last financial crisis) are now trying to get out of debt, some of these options will be unacceptable. Plus, you might not have enough equity in your home to qualify for additional funds. Remember, all banks—including those that are locally owned—are very conservative with their money, and prefer lending to borrowers with ample collateral.

Additionally, credit cards—even those nominally issued by a local bank or credit union—suck many of your repayment dollars outside the community. It's good to find local alternatives.

Finally, remember that if you take a loan from friends or family and promise to pay it back with interest, the law considers that transaction a security. Most states don't require exhaustive paperwork for transactions among friends and family, but different states define these "preexisting relationships" differently.

Boswellness Partners Tap Their Life Savings

Boswellness is a Vermont company offering certified organic essential oils, as well as resin and hydrosol, derived from the Boswellia and Commiphora trees in the self-declared independent state of Somaliland. These products are more commonly known as frankincense and myrrh. The oils can be used as perfume, cologne, incense, or for aromatherapy. The resins have anti-inflammatory properties when consumed through teas or baking, as do the oils when rubbed onto a

sore part of the body. In addition, the derived hydrosol can be deployed as an antiseptic. Some local scientists are even testing Boswellness products as an anti-cancer agent.

To get this company off the ground in its first six years, the four founders decided to tap their retirement savings. The four cashed out their IRAs (paying the penalties for doing so) and added any additional savings they had. They also worked other jobs to provide income for themselves while investing in the business.

With this self-financing (which might be regarded as the purest form of local investment) Boswellness was able to purchase raw materials and the equipment necessary for distillation. All of this was done in a way to avoid the laborious approval process of obtaining a loan from a bank. The capital and the decision-making power thus stayed in the hands of the founders.

Originally called Ismael Imports, the company eventually reached a point where the income was enough to cover the payments on a loan from a bank. They obtained a loan to rebrand as Boswellness and accelerate marketing efforts.

For more information

Boswellness, (802) 863-8005, http://www.boswellness.com.

2. ACCREDITED INVESTORS

Description

Because investment apartheid gives accredited investors the freedom to invest as they see fit, local accredited investors are among the easiest potential sources of capital for your business. You might approach angel investors—that is, wealthy individuals who might have a passion for your business. You might ask a nearby club of angel investors if they would allow you to pitch your proposal to their members. You might talk with a nearby venture capital fund; such funds typically invest deeply in just a few dozen businesses with high growth potential for five to ten years. You might also approach local institutions with strong community ties—such as churches or labor unions—that have pension funds.

Still another local institution that might invest in you is a major company with whom you do business. For example, Whole Foods has been committed to strengthening small food businesses that are its most promising suppliers.

Some accredited investors might enter a one-on-one debt relationship with you, drawn up specifically for the transaction. If you enter a debt, equity, or royalty agreement with multiple accredited investors, you may need to formalize it through a private offering (see below).

In Vermont, there are several organizations that are pooling the resources from accredited investors for specific statewide goals, like renewable energy and sustainable food systems. These include: foundations like the Vermont Community Foundation, with their grants and program related investing (described on page 35); organizations like the Vermont Sustainable Jobs Fund, with its Flexible Capital Fund (described on page 76); and investment advisors like Clean Yield Asset Management, Fresh Tracks Capital, and Trillium Asset Management.

Challenges

While almost every economic development agency in the country now touts the activities above as indicators of their support for local business, the hard truth is that the chance of any one local business receiving investment from accredited investors is exceedingly low. Even churches and unions tend to prefer publicly traded socially responsible businesses that seem to offer better returns at lower risk.

Despite accredited investors having the legal freedom and means to invest locally, very few do so. Unaccredited investors, especially those putting smaller amounts of money into local businesses through crowdfunding, have shown themselves to be less focused on the promise (usually the hype) of high rates of return.

A cautionary word about venture capital. Some venture funds, including those with the words "community development" in their title, can be harmful to community economies if they take over the companies they are "nurturing," and then fire the founding (local) management team. Nor is it helpful if, after five to ten years of support, the fund

takes the most promising businesses public, which destroys local ownership.

Vermont Creamery Partners with Whole Foods

Vermont Creamery, a privately owned company, was able to obtain a loan through one of its largest customers, Whole Foods—an accredited investor. Vermont Creamery sells both goat and cow dairy products, and has been selling through Whole Foods for more than 29 years.

Aware that Whole Foods has a history of supporting its suppliers, in 2013 Vermont Creamery approached the natural food giant (as well as a handful of other investors) to obtain a loan for its Ayers Brook Goat Dairy. The owners of Vermont Creamery were seeing demand steadily increase for their products, and needed an additional farm to meet that demand. Whole Foods agreed to help.

Matthew Reese, Controller at Vermont Creamery, says it was "generally a smooth process." Whole Foods charged 5% interest on the loan and gave it a term of five years. Then Whole Foods gave the Vermont Creamery its "Supplier of the Year" award, which increased the company's prospects for obtaining a new loan from conventional sources.

Loans like these have been invaluable to the Vermont Creamery. According to Matthew, Vermont Creamery has been growing around 10-15% per year over the past few years. The relationship with Whole Foods certainly helped it secure the financial resources needed to maintain this growth.

For more information

Matthew Reese, Vermont Creamery, (800) 884-6287, http://www.vermontcreamery.com.

Vermont Creamery's Ayers Brook Goat Dairy.

3. PROGRAM RELATED INVESTMENTS

Description

An especially promising accredited investor that might invest in your business is a local foundation. A foundation is a nonprofit that wealthy individuals, families, or companies give money to that is then obligated to use the money in perpetuity to serve the public interest. Tax law requires that a foundation give away at least 5% of its assets each year to qualified individuals or nonprofits. It is free to invest the remaining 95% however it wishes—including locally—as long as the investments meet basic standards of prudence.

You might approach a local foundation to consider making an investment in your company. Your case will be stronger if the foundation is a "community foundation," which has an express mission of supporting local well-being. According to the Council on Foundations, there are about 750 community foundations in the United States that give away about $4.3 billion each year. Some of their $86 billion in assets can and should be invested locally. Indeed, several community foundations, such as the Incourage Community Foundation of Wisconsin, have committed themselves to investing 100% of their assets locally.

If your business is related to the programs of the foundation, your local philanthropists might have an additional reason for investing locally. Hence, a foundation that fights hunger might be interested in investing its endowment in local food businesses. The Internal Revenue Service has a number of rules concerning so-called "program related investments," or PRIs. For example, the principal purpose of the investment can't be to profit, and qualified investments should offer "below market" returns. If such investments go poorly, the losses can be written off against the foundation's 5% grant obligation. PRIs thus give a foundation two bites at the apple for getting returns from its money!

In Vermont, there is a Vermont Food Funders Network made up of Vermont and New England philanthropic funders who work together to help fund and invest in organizations (including for-profit) that are rebuilding Vermont's food systems.

Challenges

Even though foundations have enthusiastically discussed PRIs for a generation, very few actually use them. Today, about one-tenth of one percent of foundation assets is being invested this way.[23] Most foundations have outsourced their investments to conventional investment advisors who have little interest in local investing. Bigger foundations with in-house investors tend to erect a "Chinese Wall" between the grant-giving side and the investing side, with the latter not being very open to the unfamiliar world of local investing.

But the rationale for bringing a foundation's investments in line with its grants is quite compelling. Some foundations trying to prevent climate change, for example, have been stunned to discover that their investors were placing their most of the assets in fossil fuel companies!

The Vermont Community Foundation

Several foundations in Vermont have dabbled with program related investments. The Vermont Community Foundation (VCF), for example, makes "below market investments" in things that benefit Vermonters such as affordable housing. In addition to its grantmaking, VCF has decided to put 5% of its investments back in Vermont. Some of this money goes specifically into Vermont companies like SunCommon or Vermont Smoke and Cure. Some goes into community development financial institutions (CDFIs) like Vermont Community Loan Fund, the Vermont Sustainable Jobs Fund's Flexible Capital Fund, Northern Community Investment Corporation in the Northeast Kingdom, and Community Capital in Barre.

The chart at right tracks VCF's investments in "impact areas" such as child care centers, food and farming, affordable housing, and renewable energy. According to Deb Rooney, Chief Financial Officer for VCF: "We see the 5% we're putting in Vermont as part of the impact we're having in the State of Vermont beyond our grantmaking, through either lending to the CDFIs or through direct investment in related companies."

"It is also one of the services we provide our donors," Rooney adds. "When people make donations to the Community Foundation, they know that we'll be looking for opportunities to invest the funds so that they have an impact. Our pool is now up to $8 million."

For more information

Debbie Rooney, Chief Financial Officer, Vermont Community Foundation, (802) 388-3355 ext. 229, drooney@vermontcf.org, http://vermontcf.org.

VCF Investments in Impact Areas

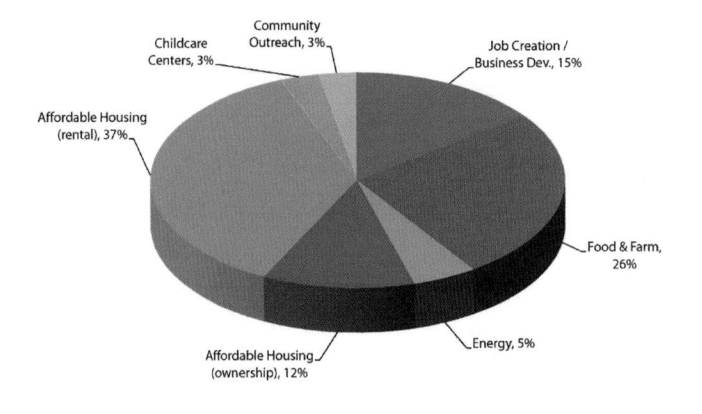

Childcare Centers, 3%
Community Outreach, 3%
Job Creation / Business Dev., 15%
Affordable Housing (rental), 37%
Food & Farm, 26%
Affordable Housing (ownership), 12%
Energy, 5%

4. COOPERATIVE OPTIONS

Description

Cooperatives provide not only a relatively simple way for consumers to invest in their community but also a tool for entrepreneurs to raise capital—in at least three separate ways. First, a company that structures itself as a co-op can amass a significant amount of capital without triggering expensive securities work. The reason is that under federal and state laws, a co-op membership is not considered a security. Co-ops can be created around several different types of stakeholders, including consumers, workers, producers, or a combination of these (a so-called "hybrid co-op"). Whenever a business requires significant capital to get started, a co-op structure offers an inexpensive way of raising it.

Second, a co-op can borrow money from its members, and many pay their members very handsome interest rates. But a loan program like this is a security, and if—as is likely—a significant number of the members are unaccredited, your co-op will have to prepare an offering statement, or "borrow" one from another co-op (as discussed earlier).

Third, a co-op can invest up to 40% of its capital in other businesses without being treated as an investment company (which would carry very expensive legal and accounting costs). For example, Co-op Power in Western Massachusetts provides discounted energy goods and services to its members—but one of the tools that it uses to strengthen its partner businesses is investment. Thus it has invested in local companies manufacturing biofuels, installing solar cells, tightening household efficiency, and making woodchips for household heating.

Challenges

Co-ops are highly democratic business structures that excite some entrepreneurs and terrify others. Every member gets one vote, and many co-ops find themselves investing significant time in electing boards, holding meetings, vetting management, and setting exacting standards of governance. Entrepreneurs who prefer working in a team rather than solo tend to find cooperatives more satisfying experiences.

It's worth noting that in Canada, the provinces of British Columbia and Alberta allow co-ops expressly for investment. Indeed, every dollar a resident put into these co-ops qualifies for a 30 percent tax credit. This kind of structure is not permissible in the United States, in part because of restrictions in the Investment Company Act of 1940, which covers all kinds of companies—including co-ops.

Cooperative Skiing

This story is provided by Mad River Glen; reprinted with permission.

Mad River Glen is the only ski resort in the country that has survived by re-establishing itself as a cooperative. The story starts with Roland Palmedo, the founder of Mad River Glen and an original investor at Stowe, who envisioned a ski area where sport, not profit, would be the guiding concern. He believed that "a ski area is not just a place of business, a mountain amusement park as it were. Instead it is a winter community whose members, both skiers and area personnel, are dedicated to the enjoyment of the sport."

In 1972 a group led by Truxton Pratt purchased Mad River Glen, and his wife Betsy Pratt took a controlling interest of the Mad River Corporation upon his death in 1975. She worked hard to maintain Roland's vision. When Betsy decided to sell the ski area, she concluded that the only people she could really trust to steward this crown jewel were Mad River Glen's loyal skiers.

On December 5, 1995, the Mad River Glen Cooperative was formed, becoming the first and only cooperatively owned ski area in America. This meant that Mad River Glen's famously loyal skiers owned their mountain. The sale of Mad River Glen to its skiers occurred in an era when the ski industry was consolidating and becoming homogenized. Mad River Glen bucked the trend by remaining independent and preserving a ski experience that exists nowhere else. The mission of the cooperative is "to preserve and protect the forests and mountain ecosystem of General Stark Mountain in order to provide skiing and other recreational access, and to maintain the unique character of the area for present and future generations."

In April 1998 the Mad River Glen Cooperative fulfilled its purchase agreement with the previous owner by selling its 1,667th share. Mad River Glen is now owned outright by its dedicated skiers. More than 1,800 individuals own nearly 2,200 shares. Since the advent of the Co-op, Mad River Glen has invested more than $5 million in capital improvements. Both the skier-owners and the management understand that skiers come to Mad River for the unique combination of legendary terrain, sense of community, low skier density, and intimate atmosphere.

For more information

Mary Kerr, *A Mountain Love Affair: The Story of Mad River Glen*, (Mad River Glen, 2008).

Co-author Gwendolyn Hallsmith at the top of Mad River Glen, looking for the easy way down. "Ski It If You Can."

5. PRE-SELLING

Description

Pre-selling is another simple and inexpensive way of raising capital locally. For example, when Awaken Café in Oakland, California, lost its lease, it needed to raise $100,000 to move to another location, and didn't want to waste tens of thousands of dollars on attorney's fees. So it pre-sold coffee to its most loyal customers, with the following deal: Buy $1,000 worth of coffee today, and we will give you $1,200 worth of coffee when the new store opens—a 20 percent rate of return.

Another creative example of raising capital from pre-selling comes from a website called Credibles, for the concept of "edible credits." Users can pre-purchase foodstuffs from local food sellers and obtain deep discounts, while providing vendors with an immediate cash flow that they can use for multiple purposes, including capital improvements, that would normally be impossible without investors.

Pre-selling like this does not require any securities paperwork in most states. It's considered more of a contractual arrangement between you (the seller of goods and services) and the buyer. If you have a loyal clientele and you need only a modest amount of capital, pre-selling might offer an ideal solution.

Challenges

In about two-thirds of the states—including Vermont—pre-selling does not qualify as a security. The other third, however, apply what's called the Risk Capital Test, initially articulated by the California Supreme Court in the case of *Silver Hills Country Club v. Sobieski.*[24] These states consider pre-selling to be a security if, among other things, the business is a startup or is offering products that do not exist yet. Note that in the example above, Awaken Café's pre-selling would not have been considered a security under this standard because the café and its coffee roasting business were operating already.

A business that engages in pre-selling also should remember that a pre-sale is a contractual commitment. It's wise to structure customer fulfillment claims so that there's never a sudden stampede.

Community Supported Everything

Vermont has several examples of businesses—including restaurants, farms, and even movie theaters—raising capital by selling their products in advance.

One of the most common pre-selling vehicles is known as Community Supported Agriculture (CSA), where farmers sell consumers their produce prior to growing it and thereby secure the money needed for the seeds and other inputs. Then, during the growing season, these CSA farms

provide their customers with regular boxes of fresh vegetables, meat, and/or dairy products every week. The Northeast Organic Farming Association (NOFA) maintains a list of farms that allow customers to pre-buy for the season. The list can be found at:

http://nofavt.org/find-organic-food/csa-listing.

One well-known case of a business raising capital through pre-sales is Claire's Restaurant in Hardwick. The founder originally wanted a community-owned restaurant, but she was intimidated by the SEC rules—so she pre-sold meals at the restaurant instead (the restaurant started in 2008 but has since gone out of business). Other restaurants that have used this method of raising money for capital and are still in business include Kismet in Montpelier and The Bee's Knees in Morrisville.

In Montpelier, the Savoy Theater turned to pre-selling show tickets when a flood ruined their downstairs space and they needed money to rebuild. The community stepped up and bought lots of early tickets to movies at the theater, which today operates both upstairs and downstairs thanks to the community support they received.

For more information

NOFA Vermont, (802) 434-4122, http://nofavt.org.
Savoy Theater, (802) 229-0598, http://www.savoytheater.com.

6. SPONSORSHIP WEBSITES

Description

Kickstarter is a website designed to support great projects in the fields of food, design, fashion, technology, games, comics, and journalism. People pitch their idea (often with a memorable video), lay out their financing goal, ask for contributions in small dollar amounts, promise small gifts to patrons (T-shirts, record albums, books, special-events invitations), and if the goal is met in the targeted time, the deal consummates. Because Kickstarter awards sponsors gifts of only token value, securities law is circumvented. Who would possibly give $25, $100, or $1,000 for a T-shirt? Well, last year Kickstarter did about a half billion dollars of transactions.

To date, Kickstarter users have pledged over $1.6 billion and successfully funded over 82,500 projects. However, Kickstarter is not a guaranteed source of funding, because only 38% of the projects reach their fundraising goals (projects that fall short receive no funds).

While Kickstarter's rules explicitly say "no business funding, projects only," the fine print provides clever entrepreneurs with a clear map on how to proceed: "If your project hopes to make money, that's perfectly fine! Rather, we're underlining that we only allow projects. A project is something finite, with a clear beginning and end." Indiegogo, a similar website intended for limited "campaigns," might also be used to fund business-related projects.

Other sites are more explicitly welcoming of businesses.

Peerbackers doesn't monkey around with Kickstarter's caveats—it's specifically about crowdfunding new businesses. Cinema Reloaded allows you to be a co-producer of a film. Hundreds of crowdfunding websites now can be found, with names like Lucky Ant, CommunityFunded, The Moneycrowd, and ChangeFunder.

Challenges

While there are examples of spectacularly successful campaigns on Kickstarter, a business raising funds there should know that the typical successful raise is under $10,000—and, again, usually for a narrowly defined project. Success depends on the business appealing to its preexisting fan base. Businesses without such a list are unlikely to win the hearts and minds of complete strangers.

Another problem is that Kickstarter, Indiegogo, and the other most successful sites are global. While they can be used by local businesses connecting with nearby fans, a truly local raise might prefer to use one of the smaller sites. Better still, use a site that has established an ongoing presence in your community so that the fans of local business A can potentially become the fans of local businesses B, C, and D.

Feeding the Moose

Vermont entrepreneur Ishana Ingerman used Kickstarter to help start her new company called Winter Moose. She had been making art out of Little Oaks Art Studio, and wanted to create locally sourced high fashion and textiles. After posting her project on Kickstarter, she raised $3,748, before fees, in just 60 days. Ishana used the money to support the research and development of Winter Moose and its products, as well as some associated legal fees.

Ishana is a big fan of Kickstarter: "It is easy to navigate the site, with much online support and encouragement. It's a nice system for connecting with donors and providing updates." She notes, however, that a successfully funded project must pay Kickstarter fees, including a 5% success fee, and a 3-5% payment-processing fee.

For More Information

Ishana Ingerman, Winter Moose,
ingerman@littleoaksstudio.net.
Kickstarter, http://kickstarter.com.

WINTER MOOSE

7. P2P LENDING SITES

Description

Another type of crowdfunding that might provide your business with a quick loan at an affordable rate is "peer-to-peer" (P2P) lending. Kiva is an online platform that enables entrepreneurs in the global south to receive microloans from people in the global north. It's inspired by the Grameen Bank, which proved that female entrepreneurs in Bangladesh organized in peer groups could be reliable borrowers of "microloans."

Because investors only get their principal back and do not earn interest, this is not considered a security—and thus has become a brilliant end-run around securities laws. In recent years Kiva Zip has made it possible for certain U.S. businesses to receive microloans as well.

Prosper and the Lending Club also can provide your business with unsecured lines of credit as high as $25,000-$35,000. Nominally the loans are for personal use, and most borrowers use these loan to refinance credit card debt. But nothing precludes the borrower from using the funds for his or her business. These loans carry interest charges that are higher than bank loans (especially for individuals with lower credit scores), but significantly lower than credit cards. Because these sites pay lenders interest, the loans constitute securities, and these companies have had to pay millions of dollars for legal work to enable unaccredited investors to participate as investors.

Challenges

Local investors will find that the biggest challenge with many of these sites is their national scope. Prosper and the Lending Club give only limited information about the geographic location of borrowers and lenders. Other competitor sites, however, are emerging that provide more information on borrowers and lenders.

The Andes in Vermont

Rock + Pillar, a trading company based in Essex Junction, has used peer-to-peer lending to grow its business. Rock + Pillar connects indigenous communities in Peru with Americans through handcrafted artisan products. According to one of the partners, Parvez Pothiawala, "the story of the artist and their heritage is just as important as the product itself."

Parvez and his partner Alma Hartman (who Parvez credits as being the creative force behind the business) were able to expand their marketing by raising $5,000 of interest-free loans on Kiva Zip—as well as generate lots of publicity for their story. The money enabled them to attend a trade show, procure more products, and do more digital marketing.

It took only about forty days for the business to raise the money from 109 different individuals around the world. Now Parvez and Hartman are committed to paying back the loan—just the principal—in 24 monthly payments.

Additionally, individuals who make loans to small businesses will receive updates along with their repayments.

For More Information

Rock + Pillar, http://www.rockpillar.com.
Kiva Zip, http://zip.kiva.org.

The weavers who work for Rock + Pillar.

8. EMPLOYEE STOCK OWNERSHIP PLANS

Description

Employee Stock Ownership Plans (ESOPs) are another form of local investment. Formally implemented in 1974 through the Employee Retirement Income Security Act (ERISA), ESOPs enable a company to give equity to its employees—and for smaller companies this almost always means local employees. There are roughly 11,000 companies in the United States today with ESOPs, with 11 million workers participating. In the vast majority of these companies, however, the workers are minority shareholders.

ESOPs benefit employees and employers alike. Employees who receive stock have another source of income from their work and a greater stake in the company. Various studies have found that ESOPs tend to increase worker motivation and productivity. Employers of companies have discovered that once they implemented ESOP programs, sales and employment in the company have risen. ESOPs also provide employers with additional sources of capital for corporate expansion, and the possibility of the founder retiring, or just exiting, without destroying the local character of the company.

Challenges

ESOPs carry a number of legal, accounting, and tax complexities, and any employer seeking to introduce an ESOP program will need to invest considerable time and money in its planning and execution.

While ESOPs give employees a stake in the company, they do not necessarily give them significant power. As minority shareholders, ESOP-owning employees still might not have a seat in the boardroom (unlike many German companies which require this). It's important, therefore, that employers and employees both have realistic expectations about what an ESOP program can accomplish.

Gardener's Supply

When Will Raap, the founder of Gardener's Supply in Burlington, had owned the company for four years, his vision and business philosophy led him to establish an ESOP in 1987—long before a well-known 2000 study from Rutgers University[25] that identified benefits of employee ownership like higher sales per employee, higher productivity, and longer company life.

"Too much of today's economy rewards capital providers at the expense of employees, especially when outside capital is needed to grow," says Will. "I knew Gardener's Supply would need new resources to grow, and rather than look to outside investors for funding I chose to unleash employee engagement and commitment to stretch scarce resources as a way to help us support a growing business. It worked."

According to Chief Operating Officer Cindy Turcot, one of the keys to their success has been the combination of

employee ownership and active engagement of employees in the operation of the business. "It's all about participation," Cindy says. "When you have an ownership culture, and work to get employees involved, they really start to care about company performance." Gardener's Supply gets employees involved in a number of ways, including monthly staff meetings, an annual meeting that's the equivalent of a shareholder's meeting, small group "town meetings" with CEO Jim Feinson.

Employee feedback is an important part of the Gardener's Supply culture. They have an organizational efficiency process that identifies needed improvements based on employee feedback. "When you hear the system is too slow 100 times from employees, you make it a top priority to fix it," Cindy says. "It makes it easy to figure out what to improve." The company even has a "brownie for your thoughts" program, where suggestions and feedback are rewarded with a tasty pastry.

"If we had not chosen the employee ownership route, we probably would have been purchased by another buyer who would have moved us out of state," Cindy says. "I'm sure they would have consolidated the call center and the distribution center. It keeps jobs in Vermont."

Companies in Vermont who are interested in exploring ESOPs can receive assistance from the Vermont Employee Ownership Center, which provides education, training, technical assistance, business assessments, and even an employee ownership loan fund. According to director Don Jamison, out of 200 firms that have taken advantage of their services, 23 have converted to either ESOPs or cooperatives in the past few years. "Our focus since the beginning has been ownership succession," says Don. "We talk about four paths—selling to employees, families, outside buyers, and managers—and attract business owners who might not otherwise think about employee ownership. Since so many of our businesses are small, we've been finding a lot of interest in conversion to cooperatives. We've done about four of those in the last few months."

Gardener's Supply was able to make the transition to employee ownership in several stages, in part with bank and seller loans that are being paid back by the company. Employees are eligible for the ESOP after one year, and the shares are held in trust until they either leave the company, diversify, or retire. If they quit, they get paid out unless the value is over $5,000, in which case they will be paid after five years. If they retire, they start receiving payments after a year. Since ESOPs are the equivalent of a retirement package, the programs must follow ERISA guidelines; there is no more risk to employees than in any retirement package involving stock investments.

9. PRIVATE OFFERING

Description

Since securities laws were enacted in the United States in the 1930s, "exemptions" have been available for local businesses to obtain investment from grassroots investors through personal contact. This investment can be in any form—debt, equity, royalty, or things in between like convertible notes.

The most common exemption is "Regulation D–Section 504," which allows a company, after filing a simple form, it to raise up to $1 million from as many as 500 accredited investors and 35 unaccredited investors. Recent federal legislation increased this ceiling to 2,000 accredited investors. If your company exceeds this number, it is then presumed to be a "public company," which greatly increases the annual requirements of reporting to the SEC and to your shareholders. Other provisions of Regulation D, Sections 505 and 506, allow businesses to raise more money, but require more paperwork and legal expense.

Challenges

If a business has even one unaccredited investor, however, it must prepare a Private Placement Memorandum, which is basically a structured business plan. A business can prepare this on its own—there are lots of models online—but hiring an outsider to do one may impose an additional expense.

The principal difference between a private and a public offering is the ability to advertise. With a private offering, you historically were only able to approach investors with whom you had a "preexisting relationship." The JOBS Act has altered this, creating a specific—though complicated—pathway to being able to advertise to accredited investors. Even when the JOBS Act goes into effect, however, the pre-existing relationship requirement will still govern sales of securities to unaccredited investors.

Seeding a Successful Business

This story was provided by Eric Becker, and is adapted and used with permission.

In October 2007, Rian Fried of Clean Yield Asset Management (based in Norwich) got a call from Tom Stearns of High Mowing Seeds (HMS) in Wolcott to talk to him about investing in his company. It was a call that profoundly changed the kind of investments that Clean Yield makes to have a significant impact on the health of Vermont's local economy. Rian told Tom to hold a spot for Clean Yield clients in his investor lineup. Tom was stunned: Without any pitch from him, here was a financial institution wanting—not just willing to consider—an investment in his company.

Rian didn't know Tom, but he knew of him. Tom and his co-owner, Meredith Davis, had started a small organic seed company. He was part of a group of young farmers, cheese makers, and other "valued-added" food producers

who—with a group of older organic farmers and producers from the back-to-the-land generation of the late 1960s and '70s—were turning northeastern Vermont into a sustainable agriculture hub.

As a startup, HMS was funded by a bank line of credit guaranteed by Tom's parents. In 2001, the company had sales of $18,000. When Tom got in touch with Clean Yield in 2007, sales had grown to $700,000—not enough to satisfy his creditors, but enough to foretell the possibility of paying them off.

By 2007, Tom and Meredith realized that they needed about $800,000 in cash to set the stage for ten years of orderly growth. The money was needed for inventory, working capital, and to pay off a few high-interest debts the company had incurred. They didn't, however, have much to offer in exchange for the $800,000. They did have equity (encumbered by debt), but offering equity was problematic. Unlike venture capital deals where the "exit strategy" is to sell the company and pay off the investors with piles of money, Tom and Meredith wanted to retain control and ensure that the company remained in the Wolcott community. Without selling out, they wouldn't have the cash to pay off the investors with venture-capital-like returns.

What they needed were investors who were willing to lend or invest their money without expecting much of a financial return but who did expect a high social return. These folks are now widely known as Slow Money investors, but at that time there was no name for them—and Tom, Meredith, and their lawyer, Eli Moulton, had no idea whether such a breed of investor even existed. But Rian did. They were the clients of Clean Yield who had long wanted

to use their investment capital to make more of a social impact, particularly locally, rather than just investing in a portfolio of socially screened stocks and bonds.

The deal HMS came up with was to issue a 10-year convertible note, a loan that could be converted into equity at some point. The note accrued interest at 6%, which for the time (pre-crash) was well below bank rates. Because the interest accrued, and wouldn't be paid out until the conversion date—five years after the note's issuance—HMS was not burdened by immediate payouts that could slow down growth. The conversion date was set as December 31, 2012. If all investors converted they would own 30% of the stock—not enough to control the company, but enough to have a voice.

If investors didn't convert, they would be paid out their original investment, the accrued interest, and interest on the principal for the next five years. Neither HMS nor the investor pool knew at the outset whether converting to equity at the conversion date would be good or bad. Initial feelings were that if everything went well the investors would not convert, but rather use their capital for other Slow Money-type projects. This was Tom and Meredith's view as well—as long as they had the cash, they would rather pay out their investors and retain their ownership positions.

Tom, Meredith, and Eli were thrilled by the positive reception to the offer. One of the first investors to sign on was a family foundation known for its work in sustainable agriculture in Vermont. Four investors who were friends and family of Tom and Meredith were also early investors. After doing their due diligence on HMS, Clean Yield came up with seven clients, five individuals and two family

foundations who were eager to invest. Fittingly, a thirteenth investor came aboard at one of the first Slow Money events held in the country. High Mowing Seeds was arguably the first fully realized Slow Money investment vehicle, and it did not go unnoticed. In fact, there was so much interest in the HMS investment that it was oversubscribed. HMS was able to bring four more investors aboard at the same terms to finance more inventory and a climate-controlled room to house the seeds, a project slated for a few years down the road.

10. DIRECT PUBLIC OFFERING

Description

The typical way big companies involve many investors is to "go public" through an initial public offering (IPO). The typical IPO aims to place a security on the NASDAQ or another major stock exchange, raises hundreds of millions of dollars (or more), involves major underwriters like Goldman Sachs, and incurs legal expenses that easily can go into the millions. The architects of securities laws understood that there needed to be more affordable routes for small businesses to go public, and so various "exemptions" to full-scale securities registrations were enacted to allow direct public offerings (DPOs) to raise smaller amounts of capital

One federal exemption is Regulation A, through which a company seeking to raise less than $5 million can involve an unlimited number of unaccredited investors and advertise freely to acquire them. An example of a company that used this exemption is Annie's Homegrown: It recruited consumers of their popular macaroni and cheese products by putting the offering statement right in the box along with the uncooked noodles. Raising money under Regulation A, however, can easily cost $50,000-$100,000 in legal expenses.

A more popular and inexpensive exemption is the intrastate offering. Federal securities law basically leaves it to states to regulate a securities offering that a small business makes just to in-state residents. The restrictions for this offering—that the company sells to mostly in-state residents and has facilities mostly in the state—are slam dunks for most locally owned businesses. When Ben & Jerry's first went public, the company only allowed residents of Vermont to invest.

Companies that go the route of Regulation A or the Intrastate Exemption sell shares directly to the public, often through their website—hence the term "direct public offering." Most states allow direct public offerings with unlimited size and an unlimited number of unaccredited investors.

Challenges

Lawyers typically charge $25,000-$50,000 for a DPO, and several months may be required to get a proposed DPO approved by a state securities office. Intrepid entrepreneurs may find ways to cut costs further; for example, Jenny Kassan, a California-based attorney with expertise in DPOs, offers lower rates for local businesses that wish to go through a do-it-yourself "boot camp."[26]

Taking Pickles Public

In 2001, Real Pickles was founded by Dan Rosenberg in Greenfield, Massachusetts, to make and market high-quality pickles from locally grown vegetables. Wanting to convert the business into a worker co-op, Dan and his future co-owner, Addie Rose Holland, needed to raise capital. But they were unsure how much they needed. They spent six months working on a five-year sales and marketing plan which outlined how the company would use digital communication and other media outlets to promote Real Pickles events, tours, and investor briefings.

After determining that they needed half a million dollars, Dan and Addie Rose decided to explore a few untraditional avenues of obtaining investment. The Cooperative Fund of New England contributed a portion of the investment through a special fund designed to assist young co-ops. The five future worker-owners each invested $6,000.

Because the future co-op still needed much more capital, in 2013 Dan and Addie Rose decided to offer non-voting preferred stock via a direct public offering (DPO). Because it was also intended to help build grassroots support, they called the DPO a "community investment campaign." Through this public offering, Real Pickles was able to raise $500,000 in just two months. The seventy investors included customers, suppliers, and other co-ops, all located in Massachusetts and Vermont. Each investor needed to purchase a minimum of one hundred shares at $25 per share.

Dan says that "selling non-voting preferred stock equity investments was the cheapest financing option—one that could mean paying investors a 4–5% annual dividend, as opposed to the 8–12% interest expected on a subordinated loan or 15% annual return for a royalty arrangement."

Since becoming a co-op in 2014, Real Pickles has seen an increase of 18% in annual income, which supports the decision to operate under a cooperative model and finance through a DPO.

For more information

Real Pickles, http://www.realpickles.com.

The worker-owners of Real Pickles.

TOOLS FOR FINANCE PROFESSIONALS

If you already are involved in the financial industry, there are lots of creative ways you can catalyze more local investment. You could help start a local credit union. Or launch a targeted CD within an existing local bank or credit union. Or put together a local investment fund. Or you might pioneer two ideas that barely exist yet: a local stock market or a local mutual fund.

1. CREDIT UNION

Description

Not every community has its own bank, and not every community with a bank has one that's locally owned. There is one powerful reason why a community without a local financial institution might want to create one: A dollar deposited in a local financial institution is three times more likely to provide commercial credit to local businesses than a dollar deposited in a nonlocal financial institution.

The general view now is that creating a new bank—especially in an era of tougher regulations with the recently passed Dodd-Frank legislation (see page 9)—could require at least $12-$20 million of capital, with hundreds of thousands of dollars of legal expenses.

But the price tag for setting up a credit union is considerably lower. According to the National Credit Union Administration, the key steps include organizing 500 initial members (if you can top 3,000, the regulatory requirements are simpler), collecting an initial member fee of $5-$25 per person, and creating an overseeing committee, ultimately with at least one certified public accountant (CPA). Small credit unions can be operated from a desk with a computer, and need not have a full-time staff person.

Challenges

While starting a credit union is not as difficult as starting a bank, it's not necessarily easy. Without full-time staff, it's essential that a volunteer board be prepared to invest enormous time to start and run the institution.

Moreover, small credit unions are run like a cooperative on behalf of their members, which means that the highest priority is usually personal financial products like checking accounts, debit cards, mortgages, and education loans. Usually a credit union must grow quite large before it has enough capital to begin giving commercial loans. So starting a credit union, while localizing local finance generally, may not immediately boost local business.

Opportunities Credit Union

Portions of this story were provided by Opportunities Credit Union; used with permission.

Opportunities Credit Union opened in September 1989 to provide banking services to low-income Vermonters. According to CEO and President, Cheryl Fatnassi, "We were started to address a gap in the market for low income, unbanked and underserved Vermonters who could not find affordable places to do their banking." Opportunities' mission was and is to build wealth, community, and opportunity through a fair and affordable financial system.

Opportunities' primary market is Vermont's 90,000 low-income households. Member incomes average 30% below Vermont average incomes and three quarters of its members have less than $25 in savings. Most have been refused financial services by mainstream institutions.

Getting Opportunities Credit Union off the ground was not easy. Established in 1989 with a $20,000 grant from the Burlington Ecumenical Action Ministry, Opportunities now ranks as a $38 million institution that has made more than $300 million in loans. Few big-time banks can boast a repayment rate higher than the 99.5 percent Opportunities reports. These achievements were acknowledged when Opportunities won awards from the Small Business Association in 2013 and 2014.

Opportunities started small and grew smart. The financial counseling service at the core of its operations grew out of a research project the credit union undertook a year after it opened its doors. That study revealed that the nonprofit was shutting out half the people who came to it seeking loans. They recognized the need for more education on personal financial responsibility, and to be able to offer loans to members who, despite poor credit scores, may nevertheless be financially viable and stable.

Opportunities is able to focus some of its resources on lending to people in poverty by issuing special certificates of deposit with interest rates lower than those at conventional banks. Cheryl says these CDs are for "community and social investors who agree to accept a lower rate to allow the credit union to leverage their investment back into the community. Our members receive market CD rates."

When the recession in 2008 affected many of the low income members, Opportunities worked to assist them—for example, by getting grants and low-cost deposits from various entities in the local community such as corporations, other banks and credit unions, social investors, and the faith community.

While Opportunities is successful, credit unions are harder to start these days. As Fatnassi says, "Community Development Credit Unions like us have decreased by about 25% in that same period due to the high cost of regulation, risk, and finding people who are willing to lead this type of organization."

For more information

Cheryl Fatnassi, Opportunities Credit Union, (802) 654-4540, ext. 105, http://www.oppsvt.org.

Receiving the 2013 Small Business Association Award.

2. TARGETED CDS

Description

All banks, even locally owned ones, are very conservative about lending their money. The law demands this. That's why they usually insist that their clients fully collateralize any loans. Typically a mortgage must be collateralized by the land and the building, an equipment purchase must be collateralized by the machinery itself, and a commercial loan to an entrepreneur must be collateralized by the borrower's house. This has led grassroots groups and businesses to provide collateral to banks as "targeted certificates of deposit" so that the banks can do more lending to local business.

Here are some examples:

- Influenced by the ideas of E.F. Schumacher, the Self-Help Association for a Regional Economy (SHARE) convinced Great Barrington Savings (now Berkshire Bank), based in Massachusetts, to create a special savings account, the proceeds of which then collateralized small loans to local businesses recommended by SHARE. With 70 depositors, the program made 14 loans of $3,000 each in the 1980s.
- The Alternatives Credit Union in Ithaca, New York, has a Community Partnership Lending Program in which nonprofits can run their own lending programs collateralized by their members and other supporters.

Challenges

With few existing examples of targeted CDs—and considering the significant differences in how they have been structured—it has been difficult to convince other banks and credit unions to adopt these models. Each requires serious commitment from the partner bank or credit union to make it work. It helps if the sponsoring institution is convinced that it's not just a do-good program but also will bring new customers through the door.

Fair Trade CDs

Portions of this story originally appeared in Local Dollars, Local Sense *(2012) by Michael Shuman.*

Equal Exchange, a worker-controlled, fair-trade coffee company, started in 1986 as a solidarity project with small-holding farmers in Nicaragua, at a time when the U.S. government was trying to overthrow the Sandinista government. The idea was to purchase coffee directly from family-farmer cooperatives. By cutting out the "middle man," fair trade puts more income into the pockets of growers. Today, the company has expanded its fair trade operations to tea, chocolate, bananas, olive oil, and snack foods, though most of the business still centers on coffee.

To provide additional capital to the company, a staffer named Alistair Williamson had a brainstorm: What if customers could buy a CD and earn the normal rate of return

on it, and the bank would use it as collateral to provide a low-interest loan to the company? Williamson approached Wainwright Bank (now Eastern Bank), which had a good track record for supporting socially responsible companies, and it agreed to create a special three-year CD, requiring a $500 minimum deposit, that is open to accredited and unaccredited investors alike. The CD is FDIC-insured against bank failure, but it is at risk if Equal Exchange ever defaults on its loan.

Defying the logic of neoclassical economists, the CD holders don't demand any increased reward for the extra risk. They are paid at exactly the same rate as the holders of conventional CDs. "What they're getting," says Daniel Fireside, Capital Coordinator for Equal Exchange, "is a social return. They're saying, hey, this is really the only vehicle I know of where my bank is telling me exactly what they're doing with my money, and it's a really great thing that's in line with my values, and for me that's worth the tiny extra risk." After three years, the program has over $1 million and over 100 depositors.

In return for that risk, the money that CD holders deposit can be used for tremendous good. For example $2,000 can buy, at Fair Trade prices, the complete coffee harvest of a typical family farm. That 5-acre farm, perhaps high in a remote Peruvian valley, might support 6-8 people. So a $2,000 CD can help keep a family on their land, providing hope that they can improve life for their children. CDs earn a competitive interest rate, too.

Even though the bank is paying Equal Exchange CD holders the same rate as it pays on other CDs, its margin is tighter. Superficially, the spread it has—currently between 3.25% it takes in from the loan and 0.85% it pays on the CD—is the same as it enjoys on other CDs. But the bank's costs of administering the program, Fireside admits, are greater. "The bank is taking on some extra work. It's really a sign of the commitment from them and their values that they're willing to do this. I also think they see it as a real plus. They include it in some of their advertisements. People come into the bank and go: 'Wow! This is cool that you're supporting fair trade!'"

"But it's not charity on the bank's part," Fireside quickly adds. "It's providing a real service to depositors, who want to see their money do double duty."

3. FEDERAL PROGRAMS

Description

The federal government has several programs that finance professionals can tap to deliver more capital to local business. As noted in the Introduction, the Treasury Department administers a program to support Community Development Financial Institutions (CDFIs). This program was initiated when the Clinton Administration signed into law the Riegle Community Development and Regulatory Improvement Act of 1994. The bill created a process whereby various financial institutions—banks, credit unions, loan funds—can apply for a federal designation as a CDFI and qualify for infusions of federal capital. The Clinton Administration also launched the New Markets Tax Credit (NMTC) program, which provided investors who put funds into federally approved Community Development Entities (CDEs) with tax credits amounting to nearly 40% of the investment. According to the Department of the Treasury, which oversees these programs: "Since its creation, the CDFI Fund has awarded $1.11 billion to community development organizations and financial institutions. It [also] has awarded allocations of New Markets Tax Credits which will attract private-sector investments totaling $26 billion."

If you run a financial institution that targets poor communities, or if you are interested in creating one, these programs can be invaluable. Indeed, one could argue that these are the most important federal pots of money that exist today that support local investment.

Challenges

Taking federal money, of course, is not without its costs. There are huge regulatory, accounting, and reporting burdens with which you must comply. And federal support is usually limited, and often available only once, which means that ultimately you still must have a viable business model for your local investment program.

Underlying all these programs is an assumption, which some now question, that all businesses linked with community development are necessarily wobbly. Poor people are seen as not having the capital to fully finance their own CDCs, credit unions, and banks. And these institutions are seen as higher risk because they cater to poor homeowners who are more likely to default, and to poor businesspeople who have sketchier credit records. In fact, however, we know from the experience of institutions like the Grameen Bank in Bangladesh that the poor actually are extremely reliable borrowers—if programs serving them are organized well.

Vermont Rural Ventures

Portions of this profile are from Vermont Rural Ventures; reprinted with permission.

Vermont has many pockets of poverty, so federal anti-poverty programs are at work in municipalities throughout the state. One organization working with these

programs is Vermont Rural Ventures, which has received official federal approval as a Community Development Entity; this enables it to deploy New Markets Tax Credits. It has used NMTC funds to finance community development projects in downtown and village centers. These projects include retail and office space, health care, downtown housing, manufacturing, community centers, food processing, and energy projects.

Under the terms of the NMTC program, an investor—typically an accredited in-state investor—makes a seven-year investment and receives a tax credit equal to 39% of the total project over the investment period. (The tax credit is realized over the seven years: 5% in each of years 1-3 and 6% in each of years 4-7, for a total of 39%). Additionally, the investor may receive economic benefits from the project, including return on capital during the seven-year investment period. After seven years, the investor can benefit from both the return of capital as well as return on capital.

Vermont Rural Ventures secured its first allocation of NMTC money in the spring of 2009, and subsequent allocations in 2012, 2013 and 2014. The projects it has completed with this funding are listed in the table to the right.

Vermont Rural Ventures NMTC Projects

Project	City/Town	Investment
Barre City Place	Barre	$10.25 million
Black River Meat and Seafood Facility	North Springfield	$9.5 million
Brooks House	Brattleboro	$11.7 million
Commonwealth Dairy	Brattleboro	$6.25 million
Community College of Vermont	Rutland	$8.5 million
Enosburg Health Center	Enosburg Falls	$1.87 million
Hilton Garden Inn	Burlington	$10.35 million
King Street Center	Burlington	$6.2 million
Laraway Youth and Family Services	Johnson	$3.4 million
St. Albans State Office Building	St. Albans	$9.38 million
Weidmann Technology	St. Johnsbury	$10 million

For more information

Vermont Rural Ventures, (802) 863-8424 x210, http://vermontruralventures.com.

VERMONT
Rural Ventures | The community development subsidiary of Housing Vermont

4. LOCAL INVESTMENT FUND

Description

Many of the investment fund options currently available to local investors require them to do a lot of work. That's because there are very few investment funds where a fund manager has done the work for them. But local investment funds can offer an investor another important advantage over investing directly in a local company: diversification. Investors usually want a local portfolio with enough differences among the securities so that for every company that goes bad there are a dozen that are thriving.

What has limited the creation of local investment funds is the same thing that has limited the issuance and trading of local securities—that is, obsolete federal and state securities law. Here, the main piece of legislation is the federal Investment Company Act of 1940. A new local investment company might have to spend hundreds of thousands of dollars just to be fully compliant with the regulations.

Not surprisingly, most local investment funds seek to fit in one of the "exemptions" in the Act. Among these exempt institutions are banks and credit unions (they are regulated by other laws), investment clubs, and nonprofits. The nonprofit exemption has been the most important, because it covers many community and economic development institutions.

There are two good examples of national nonprofits that invest directly or indirectly in local businesses and in which unaccredited investors can participate. RSF Social Finance, a descendent of the Rudolf Steiner Foundation, makes loans to local businesses or projects related to food and agriculture, ecological stewardship, education, and the arts. The Calvert Foundation issues Community Investment Notes, and then uses the proceeds to support affordable housing, community development corporations, community loan funds, microfinance funds (domestically and internationally), and fair trade businesses.

About a dozen smaller nonprofits have set up funds that allow unaccredited investors in their state to place money in them. The New Hampshire Loan Fund, for example, supports all kinds of local businesses in that state. Similar funds are the Vermont Community Loan Fund, the Mountain BizWorks in North Carolina, and the Economic and Community Development Institute in Ohio. The recently set up PVGrows Investment Fund in the Pioneer Valley of Massachusetts plans to make royalty investments in local food businesses.

Challenges

Unaccredited investors cannot tiptoe around the income requirements by pooling their money with others. Every single security in a pool of money involving an unaccredited investor must be from a local business that has gone public or must fit within one of the SEC exemptions that allow unaccredited dollars.

It's important to realize that even though these

nonprofit funds are exempt from the Investment Company Act, the securities they each issue to investors must be "papered" under the Securities Act. So every year, these funds must go through the cumbersome process of filing with state securities agencies for the right to sell their securities to unaccredited investors. RSF Social Finance and the Calvert Foundation have to do this every year in every state in which they are selling securities. Some states make this process easy; others make it very difficult.

The Vermont Community Loan Fund

The Vermont Community Loan Fund (VCLF) is a nonprofit formed in 1987 with a mission to address issues of poverty by investing locally. According to Executive Director Will Belongia, "It took 3 years to raise the initial $1 million. We now raise $5 million annually."

What makes VCLF unique is that it allows all kinds of Vermont investors—including unaccredited investors—to make investments in the Vermont economy and get a return. Each investor places money into the fund for a set term, and once that term is over, he or she can choose between rolling it over to a new investment or taking his or her money out. VCLF also offers money market accounts, where depositors can have access to the money they have invested on a regular basis.

VCLF uses the capital provided by its depositors to make loans to people or businesses that have had trouble getting loans from traditional banks. At first the main area of focus was affordable housing, but the loans have since expanded to small businesses, agriculture development, and childcare. To date, VCLF has lent out over $85 million over the past 28 years, with only $2 million not paid back. About half the $2 million in defaults was a result of the 2008 recession.

VCLF offers investors a "Social Investment Term Account," which then collateralizes loans from other sources such as the government, local religious institutions, and banks. It then uses this to support 14 nonprofit affordable housing developers.

Many Vermont businesses have benefited from VCLF's unique services. In particular, Will recalls a story about a pork processing and marketing business called Vermont Smoke and Cure. When the company first started off, it was small and unprofitable. But VCLF saw the potential for growth, and now the company is thriving.

As this handbook is going to print, VCLF has just announced a new loan fund dedicated to investing in Vermont's healthy foods, sustainable agriculture and natural resources enterprises.

For more information

Will Belongia, Vermont Community Loan Fund, (802) 223-1448, http://www.investinvermont.org.

5. LOCAL STOCK MARKET

Description

Ultimately, a healthy local investment ecosystem requires a place where holders of local securities, whether debt notes or stock, can sell them to other potential local investors. Doing this directly with just the people you know is not very efficient, so stock markets emerged to provide convenient venues for these transactions. One hundred years ago, there were local stock markets across the country—specific places where people could scream their bids and offers at one another under a uniform set of rules. Now there are basically just two such places in the United States, the NASDAQ and the New York Stock Exchange, and most of their transactions are done electronically.

These exchanges facilitate public trading of companies all across the planet that have nothing to do with local investment. There is, therefore, growing interest in creating local stock exchanges. Michigan recently passed a law mandating that the state create this.

It's important to differentiate stock exchanges from community portals. Stock exchanges are institutions where offers and bids for securities are made in real time, and the last transaction (where offers and bids match) sets the listed price. Since the securities being sold are already owned by someone, these transactions are called "secondary trading." Stock markets are fast moving and can change dramatically in the course of a few seconds. They are governed by the Securities Exchange Act of 1934.

The concept of community portals was introduced by the JOBS Act and similar state reforms. They look more like eBay than E-Trade. A seller posts an offer, and it can be days, weeks, or months before someone buys the securities at the listed price. The transaction has no influence on any other pending transaction (though traders of course will be interested in how others are pricing a given security). Right now, these transactions are limited to the initial sale of securities, not secondary trading.

Challenges

Under the Securities Exchange Act, it is not clear whether states like Michigan have the right to create stock exchanges even if the securities are 100% owned and traded in the state. It's not even clear they have the right to create community portals. While the SEC could issue a "no action letter" to permit these kinds of state initiatives, it has not done so yet.

There are clearly permissible approaches to creating local stock exchanges, but they are difficult and expensive. The existing exchanges, like the NASDAQ, have all the authority they need to set up state exchanges as part of their business. A new exchange also could file for a license under the rules for Alternative Trading Systems—a space for some experimentation in the field.

If you're interested in setting up an exchange or a portal, also remember that the rules right now limit their

operation to broker-dealers. The proposed rules for the JOBS Act would allow non-professionals to operate a community portal and also to take success fees, which might be critical to the long-term success of a portal as a business.

Milk Money

After hearing a talk that Gwendolyn (one of the co-authors) gave about the possibilities offered by the proposed SEC rules for crowdsourced investment, Janice Shade and her partner Louisa Schibli looked at each other and said, "We know how to do that." And they started planning a new business called Milk Money.

Their target audience is the 1,000 or more small businesses that are started in Vermont every year, particularly consumer products companies. Their goal is to forge connections between everyday investors, accredited investors, and new business owners to fill gaps in the availability of start-up business capital for entrepreneurs.

The first company to take advantage of their services (which include guidance, legal templates, an online fundraising platform, and investor relations management) is a start-up company that designs "lactation pods" (privacy rooms) for nursing mothers that are being installed in airports, public buildings, and other places around the country.

The 2014 state law that provided for the Vermont Small Business Offering Exemption (VSBOE) enabled them to start their business, even as the final regulations for crowdsourced investment are still awaiting approval by the SEC. This means that for now, the investors who can use their services all need to be from Vermont. They have set up a Contributions page on their website that will work like the crowdfunding sites, so people from outside of Vermont who want to contribute to a campaign can—but as a donation rather than as an investment.

For more information

Milk Money L3C, PO Box 81, Charlotte, VT 05445, info@milkmoneyvt.com

6. LOCAL MUTUAL FUND

Description

Most unaccredited investors today tend to put their money into mutual funds. A mutual fund is a special category of investment fund, professionally managed, that invests in publicly traded securities. Investors can buy into and sell out (or redeem shares) of a mutual fund as they wish, with the price of each share set by the "net asset value" of the fund. Most mutual funds specialize, which means you can find bond funds, stock funds, large and small cap funds, value and growth funds, and index funds. There are about 7,500 mutual funds in the United States, and *not a single one invests in local business*. A growing number of these funds invest in companies that are green, labor-friendly, cruelty free, or meet some other criteria for social responsibility, but none of these companies are locally owned.

Mutual funds must comply with myriad federal regulations under the Investment Company Act of 1940, but two of the rules bear strongly on the challenge of going local. The first is that mutual funds must be "open-ended." The term refers to the ability of an unlimited number of investors to put money into the fund or withdraw money as they wish. The total number of dollars in an open-ended fund can expand or contract like an accordion. A mutual fund manager has some criteria—big-company stocks, computer stocks, a mix of 60% stocks and 40% bonds, socially responsible stocks, and so forth—by which she invests the pool, and then exercises her best judgment about how to maximize the rate of return. When you invest $1,000 into an open-ended fund, the manager adds your money to the pool and continues to invest by the declared criteria. When you want to take $1,000 out, the manager has to sell $1,000 of the pool's securities evenly, consistent with the criteria. A "closed-end" fund, in contrast, is a fixed pool of money. Once its shares are sold, you cannot enter unless an existing shareholder sells to you.

The second important rule governing mutual funds, implied by their open-ended character, is that they must be liquid. By law, a mutual fund manager must be prepared at any moment to honor an investor's decision to exit. Within seven days, the manager must be able to pay cash for the investor's shares at more or less their value when the sell order is given. If a mutual fund were made up entirely of stocks that could not be resold for months or years, this would be impossible. The legal mandate of a mutual fund manager is that no more than 15% of the fund can be illiquid.

Given the absence of local stocks markets and the relatively illiquidity of most existing local securities, it would be hard—but not impossible—to create a local mutual fund today. One could set up a mutual fund made up of 85% municipal bonds, which can easily be bought and sold, and then hold local business securities for the other 15%. If you're a finance entrepreneur ready to make history, then perhaps this project is for you!

Challenges

The legal expenses of setting up a mutual fund are considerable—perhaps as high as half a million dollars to start the venture, and tens of thousands (perhaps more) every year. Plus, the managers of such a fund must obtain a number of licenses and approvals from the SEC and the U.S. Financial Industry Regulatory Authority (FINRA).

A Dream of a Vermont Local Mutual Fund

The idea of a local mutual fund in Vermont is still so new that we don't have an example to demonstrate how it works; so, here is our shared dream of one:

Imagine it's 2025 in downtown Montpelier, Vermont. The streets and storefronts are filled with thriving local businesses—coffee shops with fair trade coffee brewing, clothing stores with locally sewn fashions that compete with the best you can get in big cities like New York, and restaurants serving food that is all grown within 20 miles of the city by organic farmers who are living economically healthy lives.

It wasn't always like this. Before local investing was the norm, these downtown stores struggled to compete with the big Walmart in the next town; restaurants closed when new national chains opened and underpriced them with cheap food from factory farms; and clothes were almost all imported from distant places.

Things began to change when the state started to make it easier for people to direct their savings and investment to local companies. Crowdfunded investments took off, as people from all walks of life could offer small investments in new companies; and as they earned returns on their investments, everyone had more disposable income to spend on the new products—products that were made locally, eliminating the need for carbon-intensive, expensive shipping from countries where deplorable working conditions were the norm.

Then some creative entrepreneurs had the idea that individual crowdsourced investments could be pooled together into local mutual funds; this would spread the risk around among a variety of start-up businesses, and make people's investments a bit more stable. Several new funds sprung up: the Vermont First Food Fund, the Net Zero Energy Fund, the Arts Alive Creative Economy Fund. One of the most successful was the Fossil Fuel Free Transportation Fund, which helped people convert from gas-guzzling automobiles to bicycles, transit, and new electric car alternatives.

MULTI-CONSTITUENT TOOLS

One of the best ways to support the local investment revolution is to simply involve everyone: investors, businesses, and finance professionals. Even student activists can get involved. You could create a chapter of the Local Investment Opportunities Network (LION) or Slow Money. You could assemble and promote a list of local businesses and local investors (and let them do the talking).

1. INVESTOR NETWORKS

Description

One of the challenges of securities laws noted earlier is that even after you do an enormous amount of legal paperwork, unless you take your company public you still can only approach investors with whom you have a "preexisting relationship." What constitutes a preexisting relationship varies from state to state, but it probably means more than just being a Facebook friend. That said, there's no question that creating better relationships between businesses and investors can help to facilitate legally compliant local investment.

That was the motivation for investment adviser James Frazier to set up the Local Investment Opportunities Network (LION) in Port Townsend, Washington, in 2008. He basically organized monthly parties for all the local businesses and investors in this town of nearly 10,000, plied attendees with free food and drinks, and at the end of each event asked attendees to indicate at with whom they now had a preexisting relationship. He then circulated the business plans and funding pitches he received from local businesses accordingly, leaving it up it to individual investors and entrepreneurs to meet and strike their own deals. Unaccredited investors could participate, though it was up to each business to create a deal structure that allowed their money (or not). Because LION was not selling any securities, nor taking commissions or fees, it tiptoed around the SEC proscriptions against public solicitation.

The result of this one modest social invention has been about $1 million of local investment per year in Port Townsend since LION's founding. Since then, Frazier has been helping organize other LIONs across the country. He also recently opened a clearinghouse for local investors called the Local Investing Resource Center (LIRC).

Challenges

The law regarding solicitation is complicated and confusing. The JOBS Act changed federal law, freeing up any company to approach an accredited investor for funding. But a whole new set of legal requirements have been imposed on companies that solicit this way.

For local investments that are wholly within a single state, state solicitation rules apply—and as noted, these vary enormously. If you're interested in setting up a LION, it's wise to consult with a securities attorney first to elaborate the do's and don'ts for solicitation.

Slow Money Vermont

The main effort to create a local investor network in Vermont has been led by the local chapter of Slow Money. The term "slow money" was inspired by the international group Slow Food, which was founded by Italian Carlo Petrini in 1986 as a counter to fast food and has since spread to 150 countries. Petrini preached the value of enjoying the relationship-building quality of knowing your farmer, shopping

locally for fresh food, cooking at home, and enjoying family meals. Woody Tasch, a pioneer in the field of socially responsible investing, applied these concepts to investing in his book *Slow Money*, published in 2010. The public response was overwhelming, so much so that Tasch decided to transform his book's ideas into a grassroots organization with the same name.

Across the United States and in other countries as well, Slow Money chapters are now exploring all the local investment strategies outlined in this handbook, with the goal of placing one percent of investors' portfolios in local farms and food businesses. The twenty active US chapters, which involve both professional investors and newbies, have created thirteen investment clubs, and have already mobilized $38 million into over 350 small food enterprises.

The purpose of Slow Money Vermont chapter is to connect entrepreneurs and investors interested in local food enterprises, as well as to inspire others. Unlike other angel investor networks, Slow Money includes unaccredited investors. By building relationships among entrepreneurs and local businesses, Slow Money hopes not only to facilitate local investment but also to create relationships that can solve problems. The Vermont chapter plans to put on entrepreneur showcases where vetted businesses can present their business plans to potentially interested investors. Events like these generate not just dollars for local food providers but also social capital—which might lead, for example, to offers of technical assistance.

For more information

Eric Becker, (802) 526-2525, http://slowmoney.org/local-groups#vermont.

2. COMMUNITY LISTS

Description

One huge obstacle to local investment is information. Investors think there's no local "deal flow." And businesses think there's no critical mass of interested local investors. Both groups are probably wrong—but understandably so, because both groups lack critical information about one another.

A simple way to overcome this obstacle is to create a website listing local companies that are interested in local investors. Think of a Yahoo! Finance web page, but listing local businesses. No transactions. No pitches. No details about the deal. Just information about the company that lets investors know, if they are interested, who they can email or call to explore a potential investment opportunity. Additionally, the web page might also provide a list of local providers of self-directed IRAs (see above), who could help investors move tax-deferred retirement savings into these companies.

By providing web visitors with just this most basic information about the supply and demand of local securities, your community will establish an invaluable framework for a local investment marketplace—essentially an electronic LION.

Challenges

Believe it or not, even this kind of sketchy information might violate your state's laws governing solicitation for securities. It may be necessary, therefore, to sit down with your state securities department and negotiate what exactly is permissible. Better still, however, you might work to change the securities laws to allow free communication about investment opportunities for all your state residents, as Vermont recently did.

Vermont Food Investors Network

People who want to support local food and farms can now make direct investments into local food businesses through the Vermont Food Investors Network, a project of Slow Money Vermont (see the previous section). To comport with securities laws, the Network has different lists for accredited and unaccredited investors. Every investor also must confirm that he or she is a resident of Vermont. The group's founder, Eric Becker, set it up on a membership basis.

The Vermont Food Investors Network is serving as an important intermediary between Vermont businesses and Vermont residents. It also circulates business plans to those potential investors who have the requisite "preexisting relationship" with listed businesses.

For more information

Eric Becker, (802) 526-2525, http://slowmoney.org/local-groups#vermont.

MULTI-CONSTITUENT TOOLS

3. SLOW MUNIS

Description

Most local government entities in the United States borrow money, and one of the most common tools they use is municipal bonds—or in investor parlance, *munis*. General obligation bonds put the full faith and credit of the local authority on the line, while revenue bonds commit future revenues from a given project like a power plant. Like other securities, they are fully "papered" by attorneys who usually make them purchasable and tradable by unaccredited investors. One feature of munis that makes them attractive to investors is that the interest paid—that is, the income paid to the bondholders—is exempt from personal income tax.

Munis are often used to support major civic infrastructure projects like bridges, stadiums, convention centers, and housing projects. They also have been used by local authorities to support economic-development projects, usually corporate attraction packages that benefit non-local business. Several years ago, Slow Money proposed that municipalities issue "slow munis" to support the development of local food businesses. In Cleveland, for example, a proposal was discussed to issue "food bonds," the proceeds of which would collateralize local loans to high-priority food businesses.

While the concept of "Slow Munis" has yet to be widely used, there are a few intriguing examples. The state treasurer of Massachusetts, Steve Grossman, has issued "green bonds" to support the spread of local energy and stormwater management infrastructure in the state.

Challenges

Some government jurisdictions and agencies require special voter approval for bonds. The willingness of public officials to issue bonds, moreover, may depend on the financial health of the issuing jurisdiction. Ultimately, no one will want to issue bonds unless there's a clear cash flow to pay back bondholders in the future. For example, the food bond idea described above probably requires a municipal fund to charge banks and credit unions fees for the collateralization to cover risks of default.

Bonding an Improved Downtown

Burlington used its bonding authority to help develop affordable working space for nonprofit human service agencies. Specifically, it helped the Champlain Housing Trust develop an innovative nonprofit workspace out of some deteriorated, foreclosed, polluted, or otherwise challenged properties. The project cleaned up blight while creating a viable new commercial space where residents could work.

Central to the rehabilitation project were buildings that once housed the first Hebrew school in town. The Champlain Housing Trust used some of the space to build a new food shelf with a grocery program for families and a

meals program for single homeless people. The rest became a three-level office building, shared by the land trust and the Committee on Temporary Shelter (COTS) in Burlington, which created housing for homeless people.

The City of Burlington used their bonding authority in a way that was integral to the deal for acquisition and repair of the buildings. According to Brenda Torpy, the Executive Director of the Champlain Housing Trust, "We worked out how to make the commercial space affordable over the long term to organizations that ran on almost no money. The debt was large, so we figured out the operating costs versus what the nonprofits could pay." They ran a capital campaign to make up the difference in the purchase price and the longer-term affordable tenancy.

The Land Trust needed affordable debt also, so in addition to the capital campaign, a 30-year fixed mortgage was needed—unheard of with commercial properties that go for standard bank financing. The Burlington Community Development Corporation (BCDC) had the authority to issue tax-exempt bonds, and wound up issuing $1.5 million worth. A capital campaign raised another $1.5 million to bring the long-term costs down.

At the time (before the wave of bank consolidations) there were six local banks, so the Land Trust went to the six bank presidents and asked them to capitalize 1/6th of the total bond issue each. Based on the bonds secured by a mortgage, the banks bought the bonds, and the mortgages were paid to them. One bank acted as the coordinator and collected the mortgages. As the mortgages were paid off, the bond was paid off. The properties were built to standards that were state-of-the-art at the time, and operated on a rent control system that gave the nonprofit agencies affordable space.

For more information

Champlain Housing Trust, (802) 862-6244, http://www.getahome.org.

Procession to the first Hebrew Free School in Burlington, 1910.

LEGAL AND REGULATORY ACTION

If you are a politician, policymaker, or grassroots wonk, you might want to think about ways the state can facilitate local investment. Vermont could reform its securities laws (it's already made some helpful reforms). It could expand the role of quasi-state initiatives like the Flex Capital Fund. Or it could create a public bank.

1. THE JOBS ACT AND STATE SECURITIES REFORMS

Description

Reforming securities laws can provide important new options to facilitate local investment. This happened at the national level when President Obama signed the Jumpstart Our Businesses (JOBS) Act into law in April 2012. It created a relatively simple path for any local business to raise up to $1 million through federally licensed "portals" (see "Local Stock Market," page 60). Any investor can put up to $2,000 per year into a qualifying company, and this ceiling increases with one's income.

While the preliminary rules for this "Title III Crowdfunding" exemption were published in 2013, final rules are not expected from the SEC until late 2015. In the meantime, more than a dozen states (including Alabama, Georgia, Oregon, and Wisconsin) have created their own versions of the JOBS Act under their own authority to write laws regulating intra-state offerings (see "Direct Public Offering," page 49). Most of them, like the JOBS Act, limit the total size of the offering to $1-$2 million, restrict investors to several thousand dollars per company per year, and impose very little legal paperwork on companies. Maryland has created an exemption for local companies wishing to borrow up to $100,000 in-state, allowing residents to lend up to $100 each with almost no paperwork whatsoever.

Challenges

From the standpoint of a local investor, the JOBS Act did not necessarily create an ideal pathway. It will make it easier for companies to raise money across the country from people who have no connection to the business, which increases the probability of fraud. Moreover, the preliminary rules suggest that the costs could be as great as a direct public offering. A company seeking $500,000 to $1 million needs to have a full audit, which can easily cost $15,000 (companies raising less than $500,000 have small accounting burdens imposed on them.) Plus, it will have to pay the listing portal fees (possibly thousands of dollars), and several percentage points of the offering as a success fee. Given all of these problems—along with the inexcusable delay by the SEC in finalizing rules—the legislative architect of the JOBS Act, Representative Patrick McHenry of North Carolina, has pronounced it "unworkable" and is designing a successor bill.

Emerging state laws, which are limited to small companies seeking local investors in the same state, are more promising. Most, however, are not well known by the public and have barely been used. Many of the earliest state laws are also incomplete. For example, they do not clearly say whether securities can (or must) be bought on an internet portal, how such a portal might be licensed, whether it must be run by "broker dealers" (which increases the cost), and whether non-broker-dealer operators can charge

a success fee (which might be essential for a portal as a business model). In other words, these states will probably have to pass follow-on pieces of legislation to clarify and improve their laws.

If you live in a state with one of these laws, organizing a grassroots effort to recruit companies and investors to use it is key to its success. That's what Hatch Oregon, a Portland-based incubator, did after they convinced their state securities department to create a crowdfunding exemption. In the first five weeks, they convinced nine companies to use the exemption, and collectively they raised over $120,000.

Vermont Securities Law Reforms

In 2014 Vermont revised its Small Business Offering Exemption to create a streamlined process by which local small businesses can raise up to $2 million from as many as 50 Vermont residents. The business can solicit investors in the state by, for example, putting an ad in a local paper.

The new exemption created three classes of investors rather than the two that existed previously. In addition to unaccredited investors (called "Main Street" investors) and accredited investors, Vermont now has an in-between category called "certified investors" who have over $500,000 in net worth or over $100,000 in income per year ($150,000 for couples). Under the new rules, Main Street investors are allowed to purchase up to $10,000 in stock per offering per year, certified investors are allowed to purchase $25,000 per offering per year, and accredited investors, as usual, can purchase as much of any securities they wish. (To learn more about this specific exemption, visit: http://www. dfr.vermont.gov/reg-bul-ord/rule-providing-vermont-small-business-offering-exemption.)

Other reforms are being considered as well. For example, changes are being considered to the laws governing peer-to-peer lending in the state. Reformers would like to exempt more small lenders from current licensing requirements.

If you are interested in taking advantage of these reforms, you might contact Vermont Businesses for Social Responsibility (VBSR), the largest business association in the state and the largest BSR chapter in the country. Their regular biannual conferences are great opportunities for their members and the general public to learn about cutting-edge business practices. In addition, one of Vermont's business law firms, Merritt, Merritt, and Moulton, provides educational seminars at a variety of conferences and business meetings.

For more information

State Department of Financial Regulation,
(802) 828-3301, http://www.dfr.vermont.gov.

2. STATE FUNDS

Description

Beyond reforming securities laws, states also can create their own financial institutions to lead local investment initiatives. While many states' funds are simply economic development programs, redirecting public money to private companies, a few states have created funds in which private investors can participate as well. Usually, only accredited investors can get involved, but there's no reason a state could not open up these funds to unaccredited residents as well.

Several Canadian provinces have reformed their securities laws to make it easier for grassroots groups to form investment funds. Alberta allows consumer cooperatives to invest, on behalf of their members, in other local businesses (not just cooperatives). Nova Scotia, a province with one million residents, now has more than 60 Community Economic Development Investment Funds, which allow residents to place tax-deferred savings into these new pools of local securities. For example, FarmWorks invests more than a million dollars on behalf of grassroots investors in Nova Scotian farms and food businesses.

A state also might change other laws to incentivize participation in local investment funds. Many provinces in Canada give 30% income tax credits to residents who place an investment for several years in local co-ops (Alberta), local investment funds (Nova Scotia), or local businesses generally (Manitoba). A tax credit like this at the state level would suddenly motivate mainstream investment professionals to figure out how to help their clients take advantage of the tax credit.

Challenges

While the tax credits found in Canada could be implemented here, other reforms may be difficult to replicate. While U.S. states have clear authority to set their own rules for the issuance of local securities, it's not clear that their authority is for the trading of securities (e.g., whether they can create a local stock exchange) or for the pooling of securities (e.g., whether they can create special types of local investment funds). Michigan just passed a law to create the Michigan Stock Exchange, and a potentially huge fight over federalism looms.

The Vermont Sustainable Jobs Fund

One of the most important initiatives the state of Vermont has taken to facilitate local investment is establishing the Vermont Sustainable Jobs Fund (VSJF). The state legislature created VSJF in 1995 to accelerate the development of Vermont's green economy. It was tasked with expanding state business activity related to the renewable energy, environmental technology, forest products, sustainable agriculture, and waste management market sectors.

According to VSJF director Ellen Kahler:

> One of the core things that we're trying to accomplish is a relocalization of the economy for those goods and services that we can produce ourselves. For instance, our biofuels work is premised on the idea of local production for local use. If you're a farmer and two of your largest input costs are diesel fuel for your tractor, which comes from foreign oilfields, and feed for your animals, which comes from the Midwest, could you actually produce some or all of the fuel and feed you need yourself for less money and be more self-reliant in the process? We think you can. So we're helping farmers learn how to grow oilseed crops and turn it into biodiesel for their tractors and feed for their animals. We can't replace everything imported into Vermont, but we can produce a greater percentage of our food and fuel right here.[27]

To add local investment capital to the mix and to facilitate larger investments in rural companies, the VSJF launched the Flexible Capital Fund (the "Flex Fund"). These companies often need a form of equity to fuel growth—but in lesser amounts and perhaps at lower returns than traditional venture capital requires.

The Flex Fund is the first of its kind in Vermont to be strategically focused on providing near-equity or mezzanine financing (subordinated debt, royalty financing and/or warrants) to a unique (and often neglected) group of growth companies in Vermont. These businesses are on the forefront of accelerating the development of healthy food systems, renewable energy, vibrant economies and resilient communities, while also protecting the environment in Vermont.

VSJF believes that technical assistance and mentoring and access to networks go hand in hand with risk capital. The Fund offers access to the Peer to Peer Collaborative, a program under the umbrella of the Vermont Sustainable Jobs Fund. Peer to Peer provides CEO advisory services and access to a breadth of business and leadership networks essential to the sustainable growth of a business.

For more information

Janice St. Onge, President, VSJF Flexible Capital Fund, (802) 828-0398, http://www.flexiblecapitalfund.com.

 VSJF Flexible Capital Fund, L3C

3. PUBLIC BANKING

Description

Where is your state or city doing its banking? If it's not local, you might lobby for a change.

In 1919, the state of North Dakota set up the first and only state-owned bank in the United States. Rather than allow the roughly $6 billion of state tax collections and federal transfer payments it now receives annually to be deposited in, say, Chase Bank—where the money might support robust economic development in Singapore—North Dakota places the money into its own bank, which then re-deposits the funds in local banks and credit unions throughout the state. Consequently, the state has the highest number of local banks per capita, not to mention the lowest level of unemployment—trends that, by the way, manifested long before the recent fracking boom. The bank currently has $6.8 billion in assets, and earned the state $94 million in 2013.

A populist movement for creating public banks in other states has been gathering steam around the country. For the moment, however, reformers are focusing on a more modest goal of convincing municipalities to switch their banking. One of their prime success stories comes from Phoenix, Arizona.

In July 2012, the city announced plans to invest $50 million in local banks and credit unions. The tricky part was to ensure that every deposit received insurance from the Federal Deposit Insurance Corporation (FDIC),

and that limit is set at about $250,000 per deposit per bank per year. The solution is to use the Certificate of Deposit Account Registry Service (CDARS), which spreads the money through a network of local banks nationwide to ensure that every dollar is covered by federal insurance. The system encourages reciprocity, so for every $250,000 of the City of Phoenix's investment placed on deposit in, say, Bangor Savings Bank in Maine, Bangor Savings makes a $250,000 deposit in a Phoenix bank.

What were the costs of setting up this program? "None," according to city treasurer Randy Piotrowski, "It's at market rate, so we're not losing any money. And recently when we reached the two-year mark, we ended up rolling over most of the maturing CDs. The only real cost is internal, but we have an investment manager already on board, so it's no additional work for him." The program was supported by the mayor, the city council, and civil servants. Even skeptics lauded the fact that it was a zero-cost economic-development initiative. "It helped the local banking community," says Piotrowski, "and provided liquidity to lend to local businesses and the public in general."

Challenges

Activists seeking to get public banks established have encountered fierce opposition by mainstream banks, even in very progressive states like Oregon and Vermont. The reason, of course, is that an initiative that might move

public capital back into local financial institutions poses a threat to the bottom lines of big banks. An essential political step to creating a state bank, therefore, may be to build a countervailing coalition of local banks and credit unions.

Putting State Money Back to Work

In Vermont, the agency responsible for business lending for over 40 years is the Vermont Economic Development Authority (VEDA). VEDA was started with appropriations from the State of Vermont, but as time went on this became more politically difficult, especially in fiscally tight times. So the organization decided to start working more like a bank by securitizing its existing debt and selling commercial paper to fund future loans it would make to Vermont businesses. In this way, argues CEO Jo Bradley, VEDA essentially is already operating like a public bank.

Commercial lending for small business is risky, and a significant loan loss reserve is needed. To help provide this reserve for VEDA—and ultimately expand credit to Vermont businesses—a small group called Vermonters for a New Economy helped pass state legislation that enabled the State Treasurer in Vermont to lend VEDA and other public lending agencies funds from the state's deposit accounts. The legislation was called the "10% for Vermont Program," because it put at least 10% of the money that Vermont has on deposit with the out-of-state banks back to work for Vermonters. The original idea was also to give VEDA a banking license, so that a public bank in Vermont could use the same tools as the private banking sector.

The banking lobby successfully killed the provision that would have provided VEDA with a banking license, but VEDA has become more active in other ways. In 2014, VEDA signed a promissory note with the State Treasurer for $10 million that enabled the agency to make longer-term, fixed-rate loans for renewable energy projects—a type of financing that was more difficult with the typical commercial paper lending they had been able to do in the past. This has provided the finance for several new solar energy installations in Vermont.

Public banking initiatives face still significant opposition from private banks. Bankers have warned the state about sullying its bond rating, despite VEDA's successful track record.

For more information

Vermont Economic Development Authority,
(802) 828-5627, http://www.veda.org.
Vermonters for a New Economy, (802) 851-7697,
http://www.global-community.org/vermonters-for-a-new
-economy.

RESOURCE LIST

Directory of Co-ops in Vermont
http://coopvt.wordpress.com/vt-co-op-directory

Directory of Credit Unions in Vermont
http://www.vermontcreditunions.com/findaVTcu.htm

Directory of Licensed IRA Custodians
http://selfdirectedira.nuwireinvestor.com/list-of
-self-directed-ira-custodians

Slow Money Vermont
http://slowmoney.org/local-groups#vermont

Sprout Lenders Club in Boston
http://www.sproutlenders.com

Vermont Community Loan Fund
http://www.investinvermont.org

**Vermont Department of Financial Regulation—Small
Business Offering Exemption**
http://www.dfr.vermont.gov/reg-bul-ord/rule-providing
-vermont-small-business-offering-exemption

Vermont Rural Ventures
http://www.hvt.org/vrv/vrv.php

Vermonters for a New Economy
http://www.global-community.org/vermonters-for-a
-new-economy

Your Economy
http://www.YourEconomy.Org

ENDNOTES

1. Amy Cortese, *Locavesting: The Revolution in Local Investing and How to Profit from It* (Hoboken, NJ: Wiley, 2011); and Michael H. Shuman, *Local Dollars, Local Sense: How to Shift Your Money from Wall Street to Main Street and Achieve Real Prosperity* (White River Junction, VT: Chelsea Green, 2012).

2. It's worth noting, however, that this website, and the Dun & Bradstreet data it uses, defines "local" as a business with a headquarters within the same state.

3. Edward L. Glaeser and William R. Kerr, "The Secret to Job Growth: Think Small," *Harvard Business Review*, July-August 2010.

4. David A. Fleming and Stephan J. Goetz, "Does Local Firm Ownership Matter?," *Economic Development Quarterly*, 2011.

5. Anil Rupesingha, "Locally Owned: Do Local Business Ownership and Size Matter for Local Economic Well-Being?," monograph, August 2013. For further empirical support on this point, see David A. Fleming and Stephan J. Goetz, "Does Local Firm Ownership Matter," *Economic Development Quarterly*, August 2011, pp. 277-81.

6. See, for example, Michael H. Shuman, *Local Dollars, Local Sense: How to Shift Your Money from Wall Street to Main Street and Achieve Real Prosperity* (White River Junction, VT: Chelsea Green, 2012), pp. 17–25. Also see Stacy Mitchell, *The Big Box Swindle: The True Cost of Mega-Retailers and the Fight for America's Independent Businesses* (Boston: Beacon Press, 2006).

7. Don Grant et al., "Are Subsidiaries More Prone to Pollute?" *Social Science Quarterly*, 84:1 (March 2003), pp. 162-73.

8. C. Wright Mills and Melville Ulmer, "Small Business and Civic Welfare," in *Report of the Smaller War Plants Corporation to the Special Committee to Study Problems of American Small Business*, Document 135. U.S. Senate, 79th Congress, 2nd session, February 13. (Washington, DC: U.S. Government Printing Office, 1946); Thomas A. Lyson, "Big Business and Community Welfare: Revisiting A Classic Study," monograph (Cornell University Department of Rural Sociology, Ithaca, NY, 2001); and Thad Williamson, David Imbroscio, and Gar Alperovitz, *Making A Place for Community: Local Democracy in a Global Era* (New York: Routledge, 2003), p. 8.

9. Although recent growth in renewable energy deployment is impressive, there are physical limits to how far and fast the modern industrial economy can be weaned from oil within the next few decades. See Tom Butler, Daniel Lerch, and George Wuerthner, *The Energy Reader: Overdevelopment and the Delusion of Endless Growth* (Healdsburg, CA: Watershed Media, 2012).

10. Statistics Canada, "Firm Dynamics: Variation in Profitability Across Canadian Firms of Different Sizes, 2000–2009," Publication 11-622-M, No. 26.

11. See, for example, the SBA Office of Advocacy, "Frequently Asked Questions," March 2014, http://www.sba.gov/sites/default/files/advocacy/FAQ_March_2014_0.pdf.

12. Michael Shuman, *The Local Economy Solution: How Innovative, Self-Financing "Pollinator" Enterprises Can Grow Jobs and Prosperity* (White River Junction, VT: Chelsea Green, 2015), pp. 42-46.

13. There is disagreement about how far efficiency and renewables can go. An optimistic view is Amory B. Lovins et al., *Winning the Oil Endgame: Innovation for Profits, Jobs, and Security* (Snowmass, CO: Rocky Mountain Institute, 2004). A more pessimistic view is the report by Post Carbon Institute, "Searching for a Miracle: Net Energy Limits & the Fate of Industrial Society" (http://www.postcarbon.org/report/44377-searching-for-a-miracle).

14. Of course, nondurable goods can be made more durable through reuse and recycling.

15. Well-designed illiquid securities nevertheless can provide assured streams of value. Bonds and loans, for example, can provide a steady stream of payments to the security holder. Preferred stock might guarantee an annual dividend.

16. Shuman, *Local Dollars, Local Sense*, pp. 4-8.

17. ABC News' Good Morning America, "Warren Buffett's Tips for How You Can Make Money Now," 10 July 2009.

18. Steven Deller, Ann Hoyt, Brent Hueth, and Reka Sundaram-Stukel, "Research on the Economic Impact of Cooperatives" (Madison, WI: University of Wisconsin Center for Cooperatives, 19 June 2009).

19. Stacy Mitchell, "Banks and Small Business Lending," *Huffington Post*, 9 February 2010.

20. Vermont State Employees Credit Union, 2014 Annual Report; figures based on a study by Raddon Financial Group.

21. "Taking Action on Job Creation: Invest Michigan! Fund," Dispatch, Progressive States Network, 21 November 2008, at http:/www.progressivestates.org.

22. See, e.g., Edward Glaeser, "Local Pension Funds Should Invest Farther Afield," *Boston Globe*, 5 May 2011, citing a study by Yael Hochbert and Joshua Rauh, two Northwestern economists who found that in-state investments generated 8.62% less annually than out-of-state investments (available at http://www.kellogg.northwestern.edu/faculty/hochberg/htm/HR.pdf . All the "in-state" investments, however, turn out to be "in-state" hedge and venture funds that then invest in global companies.

23. Lilly Family School of Philanthropy, "Leveraging the Power of Foundations: An Analysis of Program-Related Investing," (Indiana University School of Philanthropy, Bloomington,

Indiana, 2013). The report documents that PRIs have grown to about $700 million, while foundation assets are now about $646 billion.

24. The jurisdictions following the Risk Capital Text are Alaska, Arkansas, California, Georgia, Guam, Hawaii, Illinois, Michigan, New Mexico, North Carolina, North Dakota, Ohio, Oklahoma, Oregon, Washington, Wisconsin, and Wyoming.

25. See http://www.nceo.org/articles/research-employee-ownership -corporate-performance.

26. Jenny Kassan serves on the Board of Directors of Post Carbon Institute.

27. Ellen Kahler quote from Michael Shuman, *Local Dollars, Local Sense: How to Shift Your Money from Wall Street to Main Street and Achieve Real Prosperity*, (White River Jct., VT: Chelsea Green, 2012).

Made in the USA
Charleston, SC
31 August 2015

About the Author

When Author Adam T. Newman was young, he used to build forts out of blankets, pillows and bed sheets, allowing him to escape with his toys to the far off places within his imagination.

When Adam is not writing, building forts, or performing at schools, he can be found laughing with children while teaching at a preschool in Los Angeles.

About the Illustrator

Susan G. Young acquired her MFA in Illustration from Savannah College of Art and Design and currently serves as a departmental Chairperson at Pratt Institute.

Choosing to forgo sleep, Susan also maintains her illustration and animation business which she operates from her studio in Brooklyn, NY. She focuses on creating a sense of motion and emotion in her work.

This is Susan's third collaboration with Adam.

Bed sheets were tied together,
Blankets were draped over chairs,
And there were dozens of pancakes
Scattered up and down the stairs.

The emotions ended abruptly
As Grandma's book began to glow.
The forest started fading,
And our house started to show.

Tyler, you are the most loving, amazing, kindest and spectacular brother anyone could ever have. I love you. I love you!

Carlee put her voice in its place.
She smiled ear-to-ear.
Then exploded with words
For the entire forest to hear...

The frog tossed me the voice
and said, "This was a mistake."
He apologized for our troubles,
Then he jumped in a lake.

My shoes tickled the leaves upon landing.
The entire forest started to laugh.
Then we heard lots of name calling
Behind a flame-painted raft.

As we approached The Forest of Laughs,
Our chutes opened with ease.
We searched for that sneaky frog,
While we dropped towards the trees.

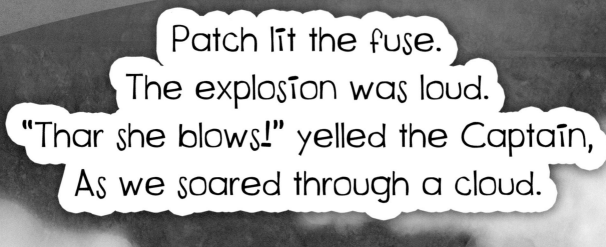

Flying by cannon is the fastest.
There is really nothing to fear.
Just wear these helmets and backpacks,
And sign this waiver here and here."

"I saw this frog you speak of.
His raft was decorated with flames.
With him was a loud bag
That seemed to be calling him names."

I told him about the frog
And how we ended up at sea.
He stroked his beard three times,
Then leaned over his boat to pee.

A Jacob's ladder was lowered.
We grabbed it really tight.
We climbed up to the deck
Just as the shark took a bite!

Grandma's book started inflating.
I shouted, "Grab it! It floats!"
It propelled us to the surface
Where we were surrounded by boats!

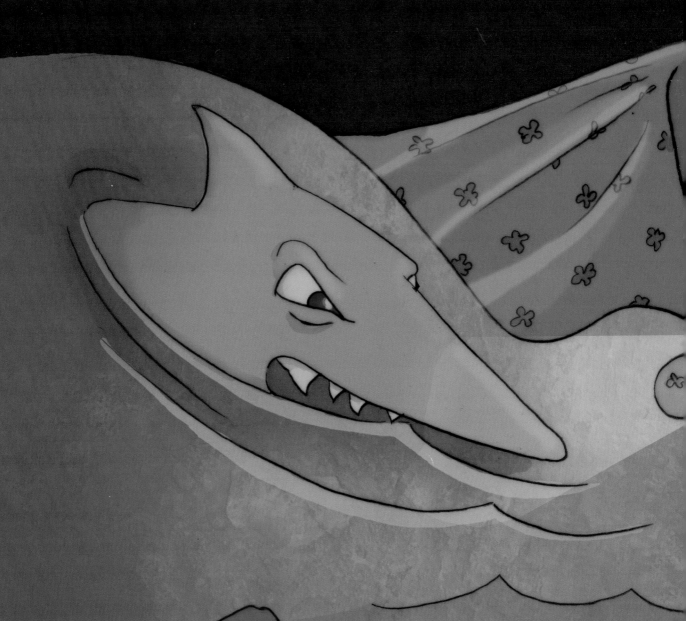

There was a blinding flash of light.
Then our fort went dark.
Water flooded the place rapidly,
And in swam a SHARK!

As we read about a talking walrus,
The ground started to shake.
The walls came crashing down.
Was this an earthquake?

We grabbed her book and a flashlight,
Headed straight to our fort,
Then thumbed through the pages
Looking for some "Grandma support."

"She once met a singing monkey
While vacationing in Prague.
Hopefully her journal will mention
A voice stealing frog!"

"Grandma left us her journal
That spoke of all her adventures.
Like the time she saved 13 puppies
Using an umbrella and some dentures."

"We need to find that frog," I shouted.
"But where would he go?
I wish Grandma was here to ask,
I bet she would know.
Holy Hot Potatoes, that's it!"

Just then Dad walked in and blurted,
"A frog took it last night.
Carlee snuck chocolate into her room,
And as she went to take a bite,

A frog leaped out of her mouth,
And hopped onto the floor.
It put Carlee's voice into a bag,
then raced out the door!"

"After, we went to Dizzyville.
The roller coaster drops were extreme.
Each time we plummeted back to earth,
You let out a SCREAM!"

No voices were lost, but I heard Gus lost his lunch.

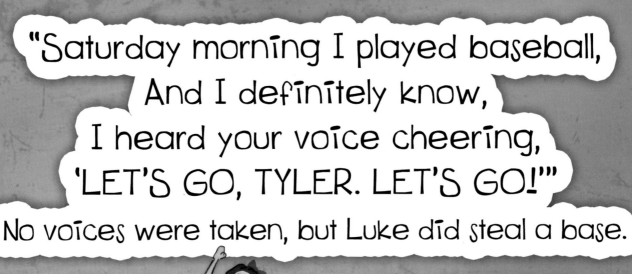

"Saturday morning I played baseball,
And I definitely know,
I heard your voice cheering,
'LET'S GO, TYLER. LET'S GO!'"

No voices were taken, but Luke did steal a base.

"If we retrace your steps
And recall when you last had sound,
We can look for clues in those memories,
And your voice will be found!"

"Friday, you were crowned winner
Of the 4th grade spelling bee.
I remember you still had your voice,
When you spelled the word Mahogany."

...It's a type of wood.

Breakfast was unusually quiet.
No teasing or fighting,
No ear flicking or name calling,
No scratching, no biting.

The Girl who LOST her VOICE

written by Adam T. Newman

illustrated by Susan G. Young